Introduction to Philosophy

UNI SLOVAKIA series
Volume 13

Introduction to Philosophy

Renáta Kišoňová

Bibliographic Information published by the Deutsche Nationalbibliothek

The Deutsche Nationalbibliothek lists this publication in the Deutsche Nationalbibliografie; detailed bibliographic data is available in the internet at http://dnb.d-nb.de

The publication of this book is part of the project Support for Improving the Quality of Trnava University (ITMS code 26110230092) — preparation of a Liberal Arts study program, which was supported by the European Union via its European Social Fund and by the Slovak Ministry of Education within the Operating Program Education. The text was prepared at the Department of Philosophy, Faculty of Philosophy, Trnava University in Trnava.

Design and Layout: © Jana Sapáková, Layout JS.
Printing: VEDA, Publishing House of the Slovak Academy of Sciences

ISSN 2366-2697
ISBN 978-3-631-67367-6
E-ISBN 978-3-653-06620-3
DOI 10.3726/978-3-653-06620-3

© Peter Lang GmbH
Internationaler Verlag der Wissenschaften
Frankfurt am Main 2016

All rights reserved.

Peter Lang Edition is an Imprint of Peter Lang GmbH.
Peter Lang – Frankfurt am Main · Bern · Bruxelles · New York · Oxford · Warszawa · Wien

All parts of this publication are protected by copyright. Any utilisation outside the strict limits of the copyright law, without the permission of the publisher, is forbidden and liable to prosecution. This applies in particular to reproductions, translations, microfilming, and storage and processing in electronic retrieval systems.

This publication has been peer reviewed.

www.peterlang.com

Contents

Introduction		7
1.	What is Philosophy?	9
2.	*Philosophy* as a Term	19
3.	Origin and Formation of Philosophy	21
	3.1. Wonder	21
	3.2. Doubt	22
	3.3. Boundary Situation	22
	3.4. Origin of Philosophy	23
4. Philosophical Disciplines		25
	4.1. Metaphysics	25
	4.2. Epistemology	27
	4.3. Social Philosophy	28
	4.4. Philosophical Anthropology	29
	4.5. Aesthetics	30
	4.6. Ethics	32
	4.7. Logic	33
	4.8. Philosophy of Mind	34

5.	Philosophy and History		37
	5.1.	Philosophy of History	37
	5.2.	Ancient Philosophy and History	41
	5.3.	The Jews and History	42
	5.4.	Medieval Philosophy and History	45
	5.5.	St. Augustine	50
	5.6.	Renaissance Philosophy	52
	5.7.	Modern Philosophy and History	54
	5.8.	Vico	55
	5.9.	The French Enlightenment	58
	5.10.	Voltaire	60
	5.11	Condorcet	63
	5.12.	Comte	65
	5.13.	The German Enlightenment and History	67
	5.14.	Herder	68
	5.15.	Kant and his Contribution to History	72
	5.16.	Hegel	75
	5.17.	Nietzsche and History	81
	5.18.	Spengler	86
	5.19.	Jaspers	90
6.	Philosophy and Science		97
7.	Instead of Conclusion		101
Bibliography			103

Introduction

This textbook is based on the lectures of the course *The Introduction to Philosophy*, which I have been teaching for several years at the Department of Philosophy of FFTU (Faculty of Arts of Trnava University) in Trnava. On the book market there are many "Introductions to Philosophy", many of which are treated as a brief history of the subject. This is not the aim of this textbook for two reasons. On one hand, presenting the history of philosophy is a much too ambitious goal, and on the other the sheer extent of this topic does not permit such an approach. I considered the structure of the text for a long time before finally deciding to split it into two parts: the first part introduces philosophy to the reader as a part of culture, in addition to science, religion and art. It outlines various disciplines of philosophy, metaphysics, epistemology, ethics and aesthetics; philosophy of mind, philosophical anthropology, social philosophy and philosophy of history. This moves smoothly on to the second part of the text which maps the understanding of history, or rather, the philosophical reflection of history in the history of philosophy (these reflections have some representation here, if only on one platform of a specific problem).

At the beginning of this text, I am obliged to inform the reader that any introduction – including the introduction to philosophy – is only a beginning. Therefore at the end of each chapter you will find recommended literature and topics for further consideration.

1. What is Philosophy?

"The question 'what is philosophy?' can perhaps be posed only late in life, with the arrival of old age and the time for speaking concretely. In fact, the bibliography on the nature of philosophy is very limited. It is a question posed in a moment of quiet restlessness, at midnight, when there is no longer anything to ask".
Deleuze, Guattari: What is Philosophy?

I recently visited several Slovak grammar schools and discussed a number of matters with secondary school pupils, including philosophy. In response to my simple question 'what is philosophy?' however, I received no particular answer. Maybe it is the fact that students were ashamed. Maybe they have weak fundamentals of civic studies, or are poorly motivated by teachers. Or, as I think is most likely, responding briefly to the question 'what is philosophy?' is a daunting challenge for secondary school students.

Jaspers argues that the question 'what is philosophy?' is a matter of dispute. (see: Jaspers K.: Úvod do filozofie, 1996 p. 9). According to Czech philosopher Jaroslav Peregrin, there are several different approaches to philosophy in society. Some people harbour an extreme reverence for philosophy, almost awe, and believe that philosophy represents something spectacular. For them it is something where we can find answers to the questions: why are things the way they are? And, what is the meaning of everything? (see: Peregrin, J.: Filosofie pro normální lidi, 2008, p. 11 – 17). Some people in turn disparage philosophy as a useless venture at a time when science can give satisfactory answers to all our questions. Neither of these approaches to philosophy can be accepted. Philosophy should not be confused with a gallery of works of art or original descriptions of the world and its sense. However, philosophy as a critical approach to reality should not be regarded an anachronism and useless. Each era, including this one which we like to refer to as the information age, calls for critical thinking. Popper introduced nine characteristics that philosophy cannot define; these are the sort of prejudices associated with philosophy (often by philosophers themselves). Thus, philosophy according to Popper:

1. Philosophy does not resolve misunderstandings
2. Philosophy does not constitute a gallery of great artistic and surprising descriptions of the world. Philosophers do not only follow aesthetic objectives and cannot be understood as the constructors of systems
3. Philosophy is not the history of intellectual works
4. Philosophy should not be reduced to the analysis of concepts

5. Philosophy certainly should not serve as a means of demonstration of our wisdom
6. Philosophy is not an intellectual therapy (as perceived for example by Boethius or Wittgenstein)
7. Philosophy is not an effort for more explicit language
8. Philosophy is not an effort to provide a conceptual framework to solve problems
9. Philosophy does not mean the spirit of the times (it is not subject to vogue) (see: Popper, K.R.: Ako vidím filozofiu, p. 70)

Further to this, Russell writes "...philosophy, as well as other studies, directs primarily to knowledge" (1988, p. 90). Solomon's contribution to this discussion states that "philosophy is not an expertise, profession, an exclusive club with its own rules and passwords. Philosophy is nothing more than thinking about such matters of life as passion, justice, tragedy, death, identity I, of course, philosophy itself, which is not at all an area nor a privilege of some small number of university-educated professionals." (Solomon, R. C.: *Filozofia ako problém? Radosť z filozofie: Abstraktné myslenie a vášnivý život: Večné problémy filozofie*, 2004, p. 25)

The therapeutic role of philosophy can be found for instance in Boethius, in the paper 'The Consolation of Philosophy'. Boethius lets Philosophy console him in the 3rd prose of the 1st book of the file *Consolatione philosophiae* when he was sentenced to death and waiting in exile. Boethius personifies philosophy in this paper; he leads a healing dialogue with it. Philosophy reminds him that other thinkers also unjustly suffered and were sentenced to death.

Anaxagoras was charged with impiety in 431 B.C. for proclaiming that the sun is a red-hot stone and therefore had to leave Athens. In 399 B.C. Socrates was accused of introducing new deities and corrupting youth; in accordance with the laws of his country he drank a cup of poison, although he was innocent and had an opportunity to escape from prison and a certain death. Zeno of Elea died in 430 B.C. in an unsuccessful uprising against a tyrant. Kanus Julius was sentenced to death by the emperor Caligula because the latter believed that Kanus Julius had known about the conspiracy against him. Seneca was similarly suspected of conspiracy by the emperor Nero, who forced him to commit suicide. Nero accused Marcius Barea Soranus of helping the coup in Asia Minor. It is not quite clear why Boethius introduced these personalities and events as a counterpart to his own misfortune, however in the first three personalities some parallels are apparent: they were prominent philosophers who died because they did not want to decry their philosophical and moral convictions (similarly, Boethius saw the main cause of his convictions in his philosophical views).

Boethius philosophy reiterates: "Thinkest thou that now, for the first time in an evil age, Wisdom hath been assailed by peril? Did I not often in days of old, before my servant Plato lived, wage stern warfare with the rashness of folly? In his lifetime, too, Socrates, his master, won with my aid the victory of an unjust death... It may be thou knowest not of the banishment of Anaxagoras, of the poison draught of Socrates, nor of Zeno's torturing, because these things happened in a distant country; yet mightest thou have learnt the fate of Arrius, of Seneca, of Soranus, whose stories are neither old nor unknown to fame." (BOËTHIUS, A. M. S.: *Filosofie utěšitelkou*. In: *Boëthius. Poslední Říman*. 1982, p. 53)

It is perfectly obvious that while writing his philosophical testament Boethius considered the sum of everything he had encountered during his life and thus the Platonic, Aristotelian and Stoic schools. The aforementioned teachings formed a background in the search for an answer to the question *"... not an abstract one at all but a very live one – to the question if the world and existence have not lost their meaning for him."* (BOËTHIUS, A. M. S.: *Filosofie utěšitelkou*. In: *Boëthius. Poslední Říman*. 1982, p. 12)

The readers of the *Consolation of the Philosophy* usually understand the title of the work in a way that the author drew consolation from his encyclopaedic knowledge of philosophy. However, knowledge of philosophy gave neither comfort nor consolation to Boethius (although it participated considerably), this came instead from the personified *Philosophy*. He describes it as a woman with a very noble look and flaming eyes. The eyes of Boethius' philosophy are *"... more piercing than the eyes of an ordinary human."* (BOËTHIUS, A. M. S.: *Filosofie utěšitelka*.1995, p. 16)

It seems that, according to Boethius, a philosopher sees things in a different way; more clearly, more acutely.

Boethius continues his extended personification: *"Her complexion was lively, her vigour showed no trace of enfeeblement; and yet her years were right full, and she plainly seemed not of our age and time. Her stature was difficult to judge. At one moment it exceeded not the common height, at another her forehead seemed to strike the sky; and whenever she raised her head higher, she began to pierce within the very heavens, and to baffle the eyes of them that looked upon her."* (BOËTHIUS, A. M. S.: *Filosofie utěšitelka*. 1995, p. 17)

Philosophy as perceived by Boethius can bend down to an ordinary man and give him a helping hand but it can sometimes appear more majestic, more distant, and more unattainable for *the chosen one.*

Boethius' Philosophy reaches *behind the horizon* and escapes from sensory perceptions. A convict viewed the clothes of Philosophy as *a work of art* sewn from thin fibres of indestructible cloth. (see: BOËTHIUS, A. M. S.: *Filosofie utěšitelka*.1995, p. 17)

It seemed to be a neglected antique on the surface. There was a sign P (practice) embroidered on the lower edge and a sign Q (theory) on the upper edge. Boethius notices a set of subtle steps or a small ladder that one might climb. *"This robe, moreover, had been torn by the hands of violent people, who had each snatched away what he could clutch."* (BOËTHIUS, A. M. S.: *Filosofie utěšitelkou*. In: *BOËTHIUS. Poslední Říman*. p. 50)

Boethius always sees Philosophy as a noble and magnificent lady, a queen who has preserved her majesty even though many scholars, schools, sophists, people greedy for wisdom and answers to difficult questions have tried to seize her. Although he considers Philosophy a loyal life guide he is still surprised that the queen left her dwelling far from a usual reality and *"lowered herself"* to him in exile. Is it perhaps because even Philosophy belongs to the accused together with him? *"Could I desert thee, child,' said she, 'and not lighten the burden which thou hast taken upon thee through the hatred of my name, by sharing this trouble? Even forgetting that it were not lawful for Philosophy to leave companionless the way of the innocent."* (BOËTHIUS, A. M. S.: *Filosofie utěšitelkou*. In: *BOËTHIUS. Poslední Říman*. p. 52)

Boethius paid tribute to philosophy, to real wisdom in all his preserved works. Laudatory words can be also found in the tractate *De disciplina scolarium* where he describes how youths should be raised and educated: *"...I mean the science about which we know that it is the only one which studies what is true and what is deceptive and those who are subordinate surrender to it as to the science of all sciences. I mean that this is the female ruler who lets by means of her see-through clothes with an inwoven ladder all the mental abilities rise to the height of sciences."* (BOËTHIUS, A. M. S.: *Školská výchova*. In: *BOËTHIUS. Poslední Říman*. p. 161)

Moreover, Boethius calls it an "imperial ruler or teacher of all abilities." (See: BOËTHIUS, A. M. S.: *Školská výchova*. In: *BOËTHIUS. Poslední Říman*. p. 162) He believes it should be fostered with the greatest of care.

Let us halt for a moment at the similar therapeutic approach of philosophy. For example, the Slovak philosopher Emil Višňovský refers to the practical and healing substance of philosophy: *"the thing is that we as philosophers should scratch the place where it really itches."* (Višňovský, E.: *Filozofia ako problém? Filozofické poradenstvo ako forma filozofickej praxe: O životnej filozofii*, 2004, p. 270)

The term 'philosophy' is not only utilised within schools of philosophical thought, but is also wielded within religious systems and is even used to define a chosen way of life or an economic strategy (a company philosophy).

Points of reflection:

Try characterizing philosophy, what is it? What kind of questions does it deal with? In your opinion, is it only a redundant anachronism? If not, what kind of role does it have?

Recommended literature:

CHRISTIAN, J.L.: *Philosophy. An Introduction to The Art of Wondering.* WADSWORTH Cengage Learning, 2012.

SOLOMON, R., Higgins, K.: *The Big Questions. A Short Introduction to Philosophy.* WADSWORTH Cengage Learning, 2014.

2. *Philosophy* as a Term

Let us start with an analysis of the term *philosophy*. Heidegger claims that if we do not use the term philosophy and instead listen attentively to the original sound, we will hear the Greek word *filosofia*. (see: Heidegger, M.: *Co je to- filosofie?*, p. 117)

"The word filosofia tells us that philosophy is something that determines the existence of the Greeks. And not only this – filosofia determines also the innermost basic feature of the history of Western Europe." (Heidegger, M.: *Co je to- filosofie?*, p. 117)

The term philosophy originates in Greek and consists of the words *filein* and *sofos*. The word *filein* translates to *sisterly love* or *friendship*, whilst *sofia* means skilfulness, agility, knowledge, cognition, wisdom, and the art of living. Philosophy could be *love of knowledge* or even more precisely *love of cognition* since philosophy does not represent anything complete or permanently fixed, but rather a process of asking questions and seeking answers.

Jaspers analyses the term *filosof* as the opposite of the term *sofos*. *Filosofos* means 'one who loves knowledge' whereas *sofos* is one who has knowledge readily available (or believes that he does) and is called the cognizing one. (see: Jaspers, K.: Úvod do filozofie, 1996, p. 12) In Jaspers' opinion *"this meaning of the word still endures: the essence of philosophy is not the possession of truth but the search for truth, regardless of how many philosophers may belie it with their dogmatism, that is, with a body of didactic principles purporting to be definitive and complete. Philosophy means to be on the way."* (Jaspers, K.: Úvod do filozofie, 1996, p. 12)

Points of reflection:

Try finding various equivalents of philosophy in foreign languages and their relevant analysis in literature. Do you know who allegedly used the term *filosofia/philosophy* first?

Recommended literature:

HEIDEGGER, M.: *Co je to – filosofie?* In: Básnicky bydlí člověk, OIKOYMENH, Praha, 2006.
JASPERS, K.. Way to Wisdom: An Introduction to Philosophy. Martino Fine Books, 2015.

3. Origin and Formation of Philosophy

3.1. Wonder

What are the wellsprings of philosophy? Where does it take its stimuli from? According to Plato and Aristotle, the wellspring of philosophizing is *wonder*. People philosophized to escape from ignorance. (Aristotle: Metaphysics, I, 2, 982 b) We are astonished by the world around us, we wonder and then ask questions, we investigate. Our predecessors were astonished by the change from day to night, the changing of seasons, the fact that one year is plentiful and another is not and this enriched their knowledge. *"To wonder means leading to knowledge."* (Jaspers, K.: Úvod do filozofie, 1996, p. 15). When we stop wondering we will start to stagnate. We stop creating and stop looking for answers.

3.2. Doubt

Doubt seems to be another wellspring of philosophy. The world of everyday experience indicates to a man that knowledge mediated by our senses and our reason is not infallible or apodictically applicable. This is the reason why man tries to criticise the results of experience. Doubt as a wellspring of philosophy does not necessarily have to lead us to an absolute of scepticism. Authors like Augustine or Descartes found a way in doubt that led them to an indubitable base.

3.3. Boundary Situations

There are situations which we pass by without noticing. An alarm clock goes off in the morning, we turn it off and run to work, to school, and then we do the shopping on the way home from work and take the children to their extra-curricular activities, and so on. Everyday routine. But there are also situations which can disturb this routine. They shake our firm ground and we have to look for support, values and answers. These situations are called *boundary situations* in philosophy (and psychology). Existentialists define boundary situations as the death of a close friend or relative, absolute boredom, serious illness, death encounter but also falling in love, healing, child birth and hope. In our everyday hurry to work and provide, we close our eyes to such situations; we do not want to see that we are mortal beings, that we are condemned to ignorance. According to Pieper, to philosophise means stepping out from the world of work, to not belong to the world of consumption, abilities, needs and gain (see: Pieper, J.: *Co znamená filosofovat?* 2007, 15)

"To sum up: the origin of philosophy is to be sought in wonder, in doubt, in a sense of forsakenness. In any case it begins with an inner upheaval, which determines its goal." (Jaspers, K.: Úvod do filozofie, 1996, p. 19)

3.4. Origin of Philosophy

As previously mentioned during our analysis of the term philosophy, our philosophy itself is based on an ancient tradition. (see Patočka, J.: *Vznik filosofie, p. 108*) Patočka sees the prerequisites for the formation of philosophy firstly in the free spirit of the Greek *polis* and its intersection with other oriental civilizations and secondly in mythological Greek religion. (see Patočka, J.: *Vznik filosofie, p. 108*)

The myth preceded philosophy. According to Patočka, living in myths meant to have the questions of life solved (even before man could ask them). *"At the moment when chaos, infinity, everything embracing ceased to be only a picture, an ordinary piece of narration with a happy end, when its insistence is understood and measures are taken to uncover and analyse it, the philosophy can be born. At this moment a new life feeling arises, from which the philosophy grows."* (Patočka, J.: *Vznik filosofie, p. 114*)

There is a fine line between philosophy and myth. Although they both take into account the being of man as a whole, wonder is only characteristic of the philosophical approach to this problem. The mythological approach does not actually have a problem, everything is clear and defined.

Points of reflection:

Try finding different sources of philosophy to the ones presented in the passage. What brought you to philosophy? What brought you to this Introduction to Philosophy?

Recommended literature:

PAULSEN, F.: Introduction to Philosophy. Kessinger Publishing, 2006.
PIEPER, J.: For the Love of Wisdom. Essays on the Nature of Philosophy. Hamburg, 2004.

4. Philosophical Disciplines

Philosophy is a collection of various fields. It consists of the history of philosophy and individual disciplines dealing with many diverse interconnected problems.

4.1 Metaphysics

It is not easy to define metaphysics. Its importance, methods and precise content have changed over the course of history. It was delineated in relation to science, theology and later within philosophy to non-metaphysical philosophical conceptions. The term metaphysics is of Greek origin (*ta meta, ta fysika*, the thing which is behind physics). This term was documented for the first time in the texts of a Peripatetic Nicolaus of Damascus (born probably in 64 AD), who was probably inspired by another Peripatetic – Andronicus of Rhodes (born also approximately around 60 AD). Andronicus put Aristotle's works in order according to subject where the works about "the first philosophy" were put "meta" i.e. "behind" the works about nature (Gr. physis). (see: Kišoňová, R.: Metafyzika, p. ?, 2015)

For Aristotle, for example, metaphysics is a science that deals with the knowledge of
1. being as a being
2. principles and causes
3. the highest existence (The First Mover) and its relation to the world

According to Aristotle's definition, metaphysics is:

" ... *a science which investigates being as being and the attributes which belong to this in virtue of its own nature. Now this is not the same as any of the so-called special sciences; for none of these others treats universally of being as being. They cut off a part of being and investigate the attribute of this part; this is what the mathematical sciences for instance do. Now since we are seeking the first principles and the highest causes, clearly there must be something to which these belong in virtue of its own nature.*" (Aristotle, Metaphysics p. 93)

The subject of metaphysics is categories, being, existence and its manifestations (not only being as such; a part of metaphysics which we call ontology deals with this), formation, ending, time, space, causality and so on. Metaphysics in the philosophical tradition is understood as a discipline which presents the most compact and the most basic statements about reality. According to Schmidinger, this is the reason why it became a science about being as being, because for metaphysics the "is" is the most general and most fundamental thing that can be said about everything that belongs to reality. (see Schmidinger: Úvod do metafyziky, p. 24). Brian Carr understands metaphysics as a categorical description. He says that the fundamental aspects of our thinking and reality are the subjects of metaphysics. (see Carr: Úvod do metafyziky, p. 8)

4.2. Epistemology

The theory of knowledge or epistemology (from Gr. *epistéme*: knowledge) or gnoseology (also from Gr. *gnosis*: knowledge) is a philosophical discipline, which deals with knowledge, its limits, possibilities, ways, methods and sources. As stated by Démuth, *"... knowledge can be examined from various viewpoints. We can ask a question what knowledge is, what are its prerequisites, validity, limits, what are the mechanisms by means of which we can get to it or what determines it and the like. One of the most serious issues of epistemology is the question of sources of knowledge. What are the sources of our knowledge?"* (Démuth, Teórie percepcie, p. 12)

One of the most exciting epistemological problems is the degree of reliability of our knowledge. For example, the Greek Sceptics asked the radical question: do we have any convincing reason to believe that what we know the reality of the outer world really exists?

4.3. Social Philosophy

Social philosophy is a philosophical discipline, which reflects society and social life; it is often a theoretical reflection of the search for a better world (social utopias, ideologies). Dominant topics of the socio-philosophical reflection on society are justice, freedom, essentiality in social life and relations to society and nature. Greek philosophy dealt primarily with the issues of *polis* and state from the institutional point of view, the relations among individuals were not a usual topic. Medieval social philosophy also dealt more with society in general (state/church) rather than with relations among individuals. Philosophy at the time of the Reformation started to analyse social behaviour more thoroughly (more about the history of philosophy in relation to society can be found in Chapter 2).

Nowadays, the term 'political philosophy' is used beside the term 'social philosophy'. Political philosophy is more specialized and consists mainly of the analyses of institutions and social establishments.

Political philosophy asks, according to J. Kis, three kinds of questions:

1. What is the correct institutional organization of society?
2. In accordance with which standards should social institutions be assessed?
3. In what way is the preferred institutional establishment chosen and approved by these criteria? (Kis, 1997, 7)

Both political and social philosophy are based on moral philosophy, they look for principles of the good and of justice and, unlike moral philosophy, they do not apply these principles to personal behaviour but to impersonal institutions, conventions and traditions. The significant events of each era brought questions and impulses and the desire for answers in this area (e.g. the research of T. Adorn about the approach to anti-Semitism after WWII or the definition of totalitarianism after WWII by Arendt). (see: Kišoňová: Kognícia v sociálnom kontexte, p. 11)

4.4. Philosophical Anthropology

Philosophical anthropology (from Gr. *antropos*: human) is yet another philosophical discipline. It centres on the philosophical reflection of a human, on the problems linked with answering the question who and what a person is? Other subjects of philosophical reflection of a human are the topics such as the soul, the spirit, death and the senses. Jana Trajtelová says that, *"The widest outlined question, which defines the discipline aptly, is the question what does it mean to be a human?"* (Trajtelová, Kognitívna antropológia, p. 13)

Max Scheler (1874-1928) is considered to be a founder of philosophical anthropology due to his treatise *The Human Place in the Cosmos.* Philosophical anthropology is quite a young philosophical discipline and its origin can be dated as late as the turn of the 19th century.

4.5. Aesthetics

The terms *aesthetics, aesthetic* are quite popular in "common language" and they are often used although the users are not always aware of their correct meaning.. Aesthetics is somehow automatically connected with art. Aesthetic surgery is very popular these days. *"At the present time of foreign words, which are used by journalists to look educated, a formerly used pair tasteful – tasteless is replaced by antonyms aesthetic – unaesthetic."* (Ptáčková, Stibral: Estetika, p. 5) The topics, which are dealt with by aesthetics as a philosophical discipline, are connected with beauty, art, nobleness, ordinariness – extraordinariness, the relationships between beauty and knowledge, beauty and good, beauty and truth.

Aesthetics as the designation of an independent philosophical discipline was introduced by Alexander Gottlieb Baumgarten (1714-1764) in his work *Aesthetica*. The Greek word *aisthanomai* means "perceive by senses", the substantive *aesthesis* means "sensory perception" and the adjective *aisthétikos* is translated as "belonging to sensory perception" or "the perceptible". It follows, then, that Baumgarten's 'aesthetics' means "a science, which deals with sensory perception". The "sensitive knowledge" does not concern only senses but also emotions and imagination. Aesthetics is for him a science, the subject of which, namely beauty, is the perfection of things. It brings joy only if it is perceived through the senses. Beauty, according to this definition, is not perceived through reason but through the senses. (see Kišoňová, Kognitívna estetika, p. 9)

One group of aestheticians (e.g. Nick Zangwill) believe that the aesthetic trial can be true or untrue. Others claim that the value of aesthetic itself is cognitive: it means that artworks are made, perceived and liked because we can learn something through them. Such an approach can be found for example in an aesthetic theory by Noël Carroll or (albeit in a slightly different manner) by Nelson Goodman. The idea that art is valuable as a source of knowledge was promoted in the strongest way by an American philosopher Nelson Goodman. *"The central thesis of my book is that art needs to be taken seriously as a science namely as a way of discovering and enriching of knowledge in the broad sense of the word of comprehension development."* (Goodman 1996, p. 114).

A part of aesthetics, which is specified as the philosophy of art, deals with questions such as: what is art? What is valuable about art? Why do we appreciate it? What are the artistic motives? What is the substance of creativity? (see further/additional information on the topic of philosophy of art: Graham, G.: Filosofie umění, 2004)

4.6. Ethics

Ethics is a philosophical discipline dedicated to human actions, questions of good and evil and morality. It deals also with standards and values. Josef Dolista says, *"Ethics is an important discipline because without it a human loses the basic value orientation"* (Dolista, Kognícia v morálnom správaní, p. 7)

Furthermore, Dolista claims that current philosophical ethics take into account the results of other sciences e.g. psychology, neurology, genetics, pedagogy and game theory (more information about this problem can be found in: Démuth, A.: *Teória hier a problém rozhodovania* 2013, 73 – 77)

More information concerning the topic of ethics can be found in the works by: A. Anzenbacher: Úvod do etiky. Praha: Zvon, 2001.

REMIŠOVÁ, A. (ed.): Dejiny etického myslenia v Európe a USA. Bratislava: Kalligram, 2008.
DÜWELL, M. – HÜBENTHAL, CHR. – WERNER, H. M.: Handbuch Ethik, J. B. Metzler. Stuttgart: Weimar 2006.

4.7. Logic

Logic, stemming from the Greek *logos*, can be translated as *term, science, reason, rule, ratio, trial* and *speech* amongst others. These translations are not sufficient to help us to understand the meaning of logic and its past and present applications. What actually is logic? The most general definition of logic is that it is a discipline that deals with the principles of right and consistent thinking. For example, Anzenbacher states that it is possible to contemplate at least two meanings for logic:

1. *transcendental logic* (Kant's teaching about a priori determinations of deliberation)
2. *formal logic* (Aristotle's teaching about formally correct thinking) (see Anzenbacher, A.: Úvod do filozofie, p. 154 – 158)

More information on logic can be found in the works by:
Burgess, J.P.: *Philosophical Logic*. Princeton University Press, 2009.
Fisher, J.: *On the Philosophy of Logic*, Cengage Learning, 2007.
Link, G.: *One Hundred Years of Russell's Paradox: Mathematics, Logic, Philosophy*. Walter de Gruyter, 2004.

4.8. Philosophy of Mind

Philosophy of mind is the youngest of the philosophical disciplines discussed in this text. It developed rapidly in the 20th century mainly on the foundations of Anglo-American philosophy. Philosophy of mind tries to answer questions including but not limited to: Who am I? What is the relation of mind and brain? Sylvia Gáliková writes that the main problems which this discipline is concerned with are: *"...problem of nature of mind, consciousness, mind/body relation, mind/language relation, mental representations, other minds, intentionality, innateness, personal identity, behavioural motives, etc."* (Gáliková, S.: Úvod do filozofie mysle, 2001, p. 9)

Philosophy of mind can be classified using a wider scope of interdisciplinary research of the mind so it is positioned on the border between the philosophical and scientific approach. It draws on neuropsychology, anthropology, informatics, neurology, linguistics; in a general sense, on cognitive sciences.

"The current state of research of nature of mind states is characterized by both traditional and new features. In connection with historical-philosophical tradition a polemic with physicalism or naturalism is going on and striving to integrate man's mind to the surrounding physical world. Even the re-established questions concerning the relation of the outer and inner world of man's existence is, so to say, clothed in "new suit". Who is the mind's bearer? Can

a soul survive the end of a corporeal body? Where does the soul dwell? What is the relationship between reason and emotions? Can machines (computers) think? What are the psycho-physical laws? How can be the features of conscious experience characterized? Do we have a free will? Is the soul a metaphor?" (Gáliková, S.: Úvod do filozofie mysle, p. 8)

Points of reflection:

Try formulating a potentially topical problem for each of the aforementioned philosophical disciplines.

Recommended literature:

ARISTOTLE: The Metaphysics. Dover Publications, 2007, pp. 1 – 35.
Démuth, A.: Perception Theories. Towarzystwo Słowaków w Polsce – FF TU, 2013, pp. 11 – 22.
Trajtelová, J.: Cognitive Anthropology: Selected Issues. Towarzystwo Słowaków w Polsce – FF TU, 2013, pp. 10-21 and pp. 41 – 59.

5. Philosophy and History

"Understanding the way in which people used to perceive time in the past and existed in it is the best way to understand the society they belonged to."
Le Goff

5.1. Philosophy of History

The Philosophy of History is a discipline of philosophy which reflects history. A lot of questions are connected with the reflection – What is history? How is history created? When does it arise? Where? What causes its movement? What is the meaning of history? Does it have any meaning at all? Where is it heading? What are the driving forces of history?

It is not my goal to answer these questions in this book (although it would undoubtedly be an attractive and ambitious subject). The chosen concepts of the philosophy of history will be presented to the reader from "primitive human" up to present day. These concepts can be divided into several viewpoints – here, we will focus primarily on the viewpoint of the finiteness of the process of historical development and thus whether it is possible to talk about the particular approach as *linear* or *cyclical*, and whether opinions about history and its tendencies are *pessimistic* or *optimistic*. The idea of a cyclical nature is present mainly in archaic nations, it was popular in antiquity and later in the concepts of Vicus, Nietzsche, Spengler. The idea of historical linearity has several representatives. Its origin could be traced to patristics but certain elements can also be found in archaic nations.

Most of the authors of this textbook agree that it is necessary to distinguish between history of humans and history of nature or history of physical facts – for example the history of the Earth or solar system. As stated by the historian Paul Veyne in his chronicles, nobody deals with what happens on some uninhabited piece of land, however even the pettiest events from people's lives are considered *memorable*. (See: Veyne, P.: *Jak se píšou dějiny*, 2014, p. 84)

Human history is attributed with an extraordinary anthropocentric attention since human concentrates on the beings that we *ourselves* are. It is necessary to forget about the fact that historiography fulfils the function of humanism or that history would be existential. Our approach to human events is exactly the same as to natural events: *"...we are interested in the only thing, its specificity; while this specificity is changing in the course of time we write the history of these changes, of these dif-*

ferences; if it is not changing we draw an unhistorical scene concerning the given topic." (Veyne, P.: *Jak se píšou dějiny*, p. 84)

However, there is a small "detail", which separates human history and the history of nature – specifically the *quantity* of historic change. A human changes more than nature and animals. He has culture (which at the same time means that he is intelligent), ideals, success, which he later passes to his descendants. When we talk about *history* we have in mind the set of all events, all actions in time and space. A science, which systematically studies history and interprets it on the basis of preserved sources, is generally defined as *history* or *historical science*. The philosophy of history represents a philosophical reflection of history, it does not deal with the interpretation of sources and events but it focuses on looking for the meanings and goals of history. Reflection has to accompany the historical knowledge in order to create the philosophy of history.

The issue of study methods of history poses an interesting and difficult problem. According to Veyne, there is no method of studying history because history does not require a method: *"...since the true things have been talked about, it has been satisfied."* (Veyne, P.: *Jak se píšou dějiny*, p.21) Historiography looks for the truth and therefore it cannot be a strict science. It does not set norms, nothing is inadmissible, and it does not have strict rules. A historian does not decide whether things are valuable or not, their task is to state if things happened. (See: RICKERT, H.: *Kultúrna veda a prírodná veda*. In.: Antológia z diel filozofov. Zv. VII. 1967, p. 548 – 559.)

"*Validity of values is not a historical problem, a positive or negative assessment is not a historian's task.*" (RICKERT, H.: *Kultúrna veda a prírodná veda*. In.: Antológia z diel filozofov. Zv. VII. 1967, p. 550)

The mathematical study of nature is exacting, all the processes have to be in their places. However, natural scientific research is not exact because it counts *exactly*, but because it *has to* count. But all of the spiritual sciences, history included, need to be exact if they want to remain strict. "*Inexactness of historical spiritual sciences is not a deficiency but only a fulfilment of a requirement, which is fundamental for this kind of research. A project and presence of a sphere of the particular historical sciences are not only of a different kind but, from the implementation point of view, also much more difficult than the realization of the exact sciences.*" (HEIDEGGER, M.: *Věk obrazu světa*. In: Orientace, y.4, no. 5, 1969.)

The set phrase *unfolding of history* is very often mentioned in the philosophy of history. We would like to point out that the term unfolding of history needs to be differentiated from the term *progress*. Progress is ascending, increasing, improvement, rising of values. The mention of progress includes positive (or negative if we are talking about regression) assessment. History should not ask about the validity of values neither should it decide about whether a series of changes in history represent progress or regression.

"That is the reason why the term progress belongs to the philosophy of history, which shows "the meaning" of a historic event with regard to its values and it assesses the past as something with a positive or a negative value." (RICKERT, H.: *Kultúrna veda a prírodná veda*. In.: Antológia z diel filozofov. Vl. VII. 1967, p. 552). We have to add that the philosophy of history is a distant empiric description of history. It is in its entire breadth yielded to historiography. The problems of history belong to the most problematic philosophic issues, *"...from all the philosophical disciplines...everyone, who to at least some extent knows what is going on, approaches this problem with horror... because so many bigger ones than us...either surrender to this problem or despairs at it."* (Patočka, J.: *Kacířské eseje o filosofii dějin,* 1990 p. 12)

5.2. Ancient Philosophy and History

The ancient understanding of time was that time was cyclical in its nature. For example, Anaximander believed that everything was born from *apeiron* and everything will return to it. Empedocles imagined cosmic events as an alternating dominance of two principles, *filios* and *neikos*; creation and unending cosmos. Plato approaches the passage of cosmic time in a similar way in his dialogue *Politicus*. A cause of cosmic return can be, according to Plato, found in a double movement of the universe.

"There is a time when God himself guides and helps to roll the world on its course; and there is a time, in the completion of a certain cycle, when he lets go, and the world being a living creature, and having originally received intelligence from its author and creator turns about and by an inherent necessity revolves in the opposite direction. " (Plato: Politicus, 269 d.) Plato believed that the universe persists: *"... remain ever unchanged and the same... Heaven and the universe, as we have termed them, although they have been endowed by the Creator with many glories, partake of a bodily nature, and therefore cannot be entirely free from perturbation. But their motion is, as far as possible, single and in the same place, and of the same kind; and is therefore only subject to a reversal, which is the least alteration possible."* (Plato: Politicus, p. 269 e , p. 431) For better understanding of time in the Greeks see: e.g.: ELIADE, M.: *Mýtus o večném návratu.* 2009, or PORUBJAK, M.: *Vôľa (k) celku. Človek a spoločenstvo rečou Homéra a Theognida.* Pusté Úľany: Schola Philosophica, 2010, p. 54.)

5.3. The Jews and History

The Jews considered all suffering in history meaningful: they sensed the will of Yahweh in each action. The

Jewish prophets, with their frightening prophecies and visions, many times exaggerated the punishment which would be sent to their nation by Yahweh. Eliade said that because of the prophets' effect historic events changed to *negative theophany* or Yahweh's anger. The first valorisation of history can be seen; prophets go beyond the classic cyclic concept and we can say that they uncover the linear passage of history in a certain way, not yet opened or articulated.

Unlike primitive divinities, which create archetypal gestures, the Jewish Yahweh is a real personality, who continually interferes with history and he/she manifests his/her will by the means of various events (draught, wars, famine, diseases). Eliade even believes that the Jews initially understood the meaning of history as an epiphany of God (this idea was later assumed by Christianity). (see ELIADE, M.: *Mýtus o věčném návratu.* 2009, p. 89)

When the Messiah comes and redeems the world, history will cease to exist. History is in this way not seen as an endlessly repeating cycle as the ahistoric nations saw it and it starts to appear as a sequence of events, which are positive at one time and negative at another, according to Yahweh's will. For the first time an image of the "end of history" emerges.

When we contemplate the approach to history in a Jewish-Christian tradition, we should not leave aside the phenomenon of creation. Creation is not something distant, it is happening all the time, *"...today as at the beginning – or more precisely: the beginning is also today"* (TRESMONTANT, C.: *Bible a antická tradice,* 1998, p. 23) Creation represents what we experience every day, at every moment. If we "placed" the creation at the initial point of history it would mean that nothing has been created since then and reality is only repeated. To paraphrase Tresmontant, we would change the *creation* to *making*. It is possible to produce only once. The world is not just a collection of parts which have been assembled and are now finished with once and for all. It is constantly being created. The act of creation points out that a new being is created, which has not existed in any way before. And this means *time*. (see: TRESMONTANT, C.: *Bible a antická tradice,* 1998, p. 23) Creation means that *the new* is continuously emerging. The verb *bárá,* create, appears in the Old Testament forty-eight times and the subject is always God. To create is therefore an activity reserved for God. Bárá is used in the meaning of giving rise to the new. Time is not only the rise of the new. It includes also decay, withering and decline. In contrast, history is ripening and flourishing, it has its beginning, *rešít, "and it is focused in such a way as a tree to its fruit."*(TRESMONTANT, C.: *Bible a antická tradice,* 1998, p. 32)

The maturation of history includes certain phases, *"times".* The contribution of Biblical history is seen because it can realize its meaning due to the prophets. A prophet, *nábí,* is one who understands the meaning of history and knows where it is heading. He has insight into God's actions, he understands the phases of creation and similar to a farmer he understands the ripening of crop. *"....he spoke with the wise men who understood the times ..."*(Est 1, 13.) A prophet does not see a spread-out map or plan where everything would be given in advance. Such a map does not exist. History is a constant invention of something new, it is not an unwinding of a model prepared beforehand. It follows that "the final hour" cannot be known: *"but concerning that day or that hour, no one knows, not even the angels in heaven, nor the Son, but only the Father."* (Mk, 13, 32) The Biblical approach to time and history excludes all forms of fatalism and predestination; history could not have meaning if it were only a doubling, a copy of the old and "original" model in which everything is given in advance. It is necessary to add that for the Jews history is a common work of God and man.

5.4. Medieval Philosophy and History

Christianity is very closely connected with history and several authors (Schelling and Berdyaev to name but a couple) are convinced that the main characteristic of Christianity is historicity and that Christianity is the revelation of God in history. The fundamental difference between medieval Christianity and the ancient world appears to be in the dynamics of Christianity. Berdyaev writes that it represents the driving force of history and is very different from the static ancient world. (see: BERDYAEV, N.A.: *Smysl dějin.*, p. 81)

The spirit of Christianity bears in itself an indication of revolt and resistance; it does not surrender to fate and is not satisfied with it. Wherein do such dynamics, historicity and spontaneity reside? Christianity was the first faith to uncover the principle of personal spiritual freedom, a concept not known by the ancients or the Jewish world.

The medieval period was primarily the time of God and land and the landlord and his serfs. The reign of cities and merchants, ruler and individuals came later. (see: GOFF, J.: *Encyklopedie středověku.*, p. 91) The time of gods morphed to a time of the one and only God and the Roman calendar gave way to a calendar which was characterized by the new rhythms. Decadal time divisions, which had been applied so far, were replaced by a seven-day week cycle. New periods specified by the Christian religion emerged, which gradually broke through in all areas – professional, social, political and, of course, religious. Sunday – the hub of the week – became the centre of human life. A week is divided into six working days and one day of rest. Social life is characterized by homage to God, religious meetings on Sunday and festive church services. The introduction of Sunday was gradual and achieved with long-term pressure. *"Church councils* *and Christian secular powers had repeatedly emphasized the obligation to observe Sunday until the 9th century."* (GOFF, J.: *Encyklopedie středověku.*, p. 92)

Carolingian legislation encapsulated the revolutionary new time. It is necessary to remember while contemplating the perception of history and time in the Middle Ages that Christian time (in the same way as the entire Christian Middle Ages) is not united. (At least) three types of time can be found here. The first time of the Middle Ages is a cyclical liturgical time, which is combined with seasonal rhythm. This time starts with Advent, continues with the Nativity, a celebration which was eventually named Christmas. The introduction of Christmas demonstrates the extent to which pagan time was replaced by Christian time; as early as the fourth century Christmas was determined to be December 25th instead of a pagan holiday of the God of the Sun. A twelve-day period at the turn of the old and the New Year, which starts on December 25th and ends on January 6th with the holiday of the three Magi, includes one holiday inherited from the Antiquity. This holiday lost its meaning for a long time and was only revived in the late Middle Ages – January 1st, the beginning of a calendar year. (see: GOFF, J.: *Encyklopedie středověku.*, p. 92)

A liturgical year continues with Easter, the Resurrection of Christ. This holiday is interesting because of its unstableness – the date of Easter is determined by means of a complicated procedure, which is derived from the calendar. This is followed by Pentecost, which constitutes a pagan tradition. Large royal celebrations and feasts were held and new knights were dubbed. The liturgical time also determines the time of the body and sexuality so it sets the physiological time and the calendar of sexual intercourse, which is allowed by the Church. Intercourse is forbidden during Lent and on days when a woman is menstruating. In the Middle Ages it was claimed that lepers were conceived during these 'forbidden' time periods. (see: GOFF, J.: *Encyklopedie středověku., p. 92*)

An important novelty for understanding history is the *linear time* of the Middle Ages. It is a time that the Bible states is created by God. From this, many historians deduced that Christianity is a religion anchored in history. The Biblical classification of time is predicated on Christian historicity, which divides history into six ages where the Middle Ages is the last age, the agedness of humanity. This pessimistic idea "mundus senescit" (see: GOFF, J.: *Encyklopedie středověku.*, p. 93) of the world growing old was gradually replaced by an optimistic vision of the Last Judgement.

The third characteristic of the Middle Ages is its sanctity. It is an oriented time, which originates in the creation and weaves its way to completion, which is brought by the Last Judgement. It is shifting to eternity and it abruptly rejects it. It is the time of destiny that emerges from nothingness and returns to the end. Creatures experience a dramatic end of time, which is revealed in Revelations. But before it happens Christ will return to the Earth and will rule for a thousand years. The Church Fathers and the Church were concerned by this faith.

Monks, whose time was governed by monastic bells, gained of control of medieval time; daily monkish time was here to stay. It later served as a model for all the subsequent arrangements of time: prayer time, food time, work time etc. *"In the twelfth century Elucidarium is created, a handbook of good Christian behaviour, which offers a very well arranged day plan: waking up, work, food, rest and social life."* (GOFF, J.: *Encyklopedie středověku.*, p. 95)

High scholasticism defined time in relation to Aristotle's teaching as a *number of movement.* Time reflections are affected by measuring and number which leads to important consequences in the area of music and it is manifested in a new style ars nova. The topic of working time is also interesting. Night work was forbidden during this period and it could be justified by the fact that artificial light was still very weak. However, fear of night work was prevalent due to superstitions; the fear of witches and the devil and the status of darkness as the symbol of sin. A new type of time could also be seen at universities, which were conveniences of the Middle Ages, – a time of idleness, *otium* – professorial vacation. Time became a social and political interest – e.g. working hours are at the centre of social struggles, merchants tried to deliver parcels ahead of time.

There are a lot of moments, which either implicitly or explicitly influence the understanding of time in the Middle Ages. Their common quality is an idea of historic meaningfulness (which actually remains at the fore of theism). No matter how confused, hopeless and accidental human activities appear, the medieval concept provides a clear explanation and they can be integrated into a history chain with a specific beginning and end. The inception is naturally characterized by God's creation and the end by the Last Judgement. For some thinkers (e.g. Schelling or Berdyaev) Christianity is the very basis for the philosophy of history because it brought the idea of eschatology or 'unrepeatedness', it unrolled and deconstructed the idea of historicity, legitimacy and meaning of history.

5.5. St. Augustine

The first truly important concept of the philosophy of history, which was presented by St. Aurelius Augustine (354 – 430) in his work, belongs to the Christian period and to a certain extent predetermines the following historical-philosophical exploration. This concept falls into one of the most crucial moments in the history of mankind when after the conquest of Rome in 410 the disintegration of the antique world began. (see BERDYAEV, N.A.: *Smysl dějin., p. 13*) St. Augustine dealt with the problem in the 11th book *Confessions*. He suggests that it is not possible to separate time from consciousness, that the memory of soul draws us to the past. But that what used to be is no more. The future exists for us in a form of anticipation. What should be, what will be is not yet. The present is still sinking to the past. According to Augustine, the present actually does not exist. So what keeps our time consciousness? The soul. It creates a subjective time flow and holds the past, present and future together in the continuum. Time exists in parallel with the creation of the world, it did not exist before.

Typically for Augustine (and the medieval period) understanding of time and history is an individual's freedom of will, which was given to him by God at creation. In history a human is not deprived of freedom. He is constantly free to choose between good and evil. History is for Augustine a fight between good and evil, light and dark. The final state, towards which mankind is heading in the historic fight between *God's State* and *the Devil's Empire*, is seen by Augustine in the final blessedness. Good finally wins. The fight between God's State and the Devil's Empire is based on a different way of loving – the earthly empire manifests love as egoism, whereas the heavenly empire establishes love to God. Augustine was convinced that all people are burdened with inherited sin, they are sinful by their nature and they will die. Death is a punishment for sin. The pardoned ones will create God's state at the end of history and the earthly state will cease to exist. The church is almost an imperfect reproduction of God's state; it assembles those who are predestined for eternal salvation, and there is no other salvation.

Augustine's conception is irreplaceable for the further understanding of history and time in philosophy since it is generally the first eschatological (i.e. bound for something – in the case of Augustine, bound for the second arrival of Christ and the Last Judgement) concept of the development of the world and mankind.

5.6. Renaissance Philosophy

Machiavelli

Niccolò di Bernardo dei Machiavelli (1469 – 1527) confirms unequivocally in his conception the idea that history and "earthly matters" in general are managed by humans and not by God. For Machiavelli history does not represent one story, which is happening in the background of God's plan. We should rather learn a lesson from history, principles, laws, which would help rulers administer their countries and which would contribute to the overall benefit of mankind. A ruler should, according to Machiavelli, study primarily history, if somebody has power historical knowledge is necessary: *"But to exercise the intellect the prince should read histories, and study there the actions of illustrious men, to see how they have borne themselves in war, to examine the causes of their victories and defeat, so as to avoid the latter and imitate the former;"* (MACHIAVELLI, N.: *The Prince.*, p. 110)

Machiavelli says that God does not play any role in history, by his own words, he tries to avoid the comfortable conclusions that if earthly events are controlled by God then each effort is in vain and we should submit to his will: *"nevertheless, not to extinguish our free will, I hold it to be true that Fortune is the arbiter of one-half of our actions, but that she still leaves us to direct the other half."* (MACHIAVELLI, N.: *The Prince.*, p. 165)

Machiavelli does not see any final salvation or reward in history or the historical process and he is not an advocate of a myth of human perfection (which comes into play in the Enlightenment). He does not even believe in any ideal state establishment or in the possibility of securing progress in the future. He does not search for meaning in history, but rather encourages rulers and all who participate in the functions of a country to use it according to Cicero. "Historia magistra vitae". In his concept we can notice a certain admission of the anticipation of future events by means of knowledge which we assume from the reflection of the past. The human spirit acts as the driving force of history. Political spheres play an important role in history. It is the very political scene which conditions the direction in which the entire historical process moves. It is necessary to mention here that Machiavelli's theory of historic relationships, which he derived from political facts, is one of the first referring to the irreplaceable function of politics in history.

5.7. Modern Philosophy and History

Modern history brought secularization, a gradual differentiation of all areas of life, and independence in science, art, and agriculture. After medieval theocentricity the understanding of historical anthropocentrism begins to come to the fore. A question of topicality and historicity of a human forms one of the main topics in modern European philosophy. It concentrates on *human fate* and primarily on a person's topicality, dependence (historic, social, physiological...), place in history and their own individual history. Science is an important phenomenon of modern history (see: HEIDEGGER, M.: *Věk obrazu světa*.In: Orientace, y.4, no. 5, p. 64) that has significantly influenced the concept of the philosophy of history. Among other things, Heidegger dealt with research into the formation of the modern epoch and concluded that, in addition to science, machinery and dedivinitization are also key phenomena. (see: HEIDEGGER, M.: *Věk obrazu světa*.In: Orientace, y.4, no. 5, p. 64) Dedivinitization plays a major role when creating philosophical reflections of history. We should bear in mind that with dedivinitization Heidegger does not mean elimination of gods and God but *"ordinary"* atheism. *"The loss of the gods is a twofold process. On the one hand, the world picture is Christianized inasmuch as the cause of the world is posited as infinite, unconditional, absolute. On the other hand, Christendom transforms Christian doctrine into a world view. "* (see: HEIDEGGER, M.: *Věk obrazu světa.* In: Orientace, y.4, no. 5, p. 64) According to Heidegger, the emptiness, which emerged after losing the gods, is filled with historical research of the myth.

5.8. Vico

A Neapolitan, Giambattistan Vico (1668-1744), is considered by many authors to be the first real philosopher of history. We can call him the creator of the modern theory of cyclical development, nations and cultures. He presented this theory in the treatise *The New Science*. The title paraphrases the key treatise of Vico's favourite thinker – Francis Bacon and his *New Organon*. According to Vico, society develops on the basis of inner rules and even behind seemingly historic chaos we can find rational order. Vico divides history (as do many other authors) into history which concerns nature and history which concerns mankind. The subject of Vico's research is the history of mankind. The reason comes from Vico's theory of knowledge – history is the result of actions and it is characterized by recognisability. God created nature so it is only He who truly knows it. Vico considers historical knowledge superior to natural scientific knowledge. The historical knowledge can be, in his opinion, interpreted as consciousness of mankind about its own creative activities. (see: LEMON, M.C.: *Philosophy of History*, pp. 131-133)

Vico's concept does not support scholastic philosophy but he finds inspiration in the work of Francis Bacon and in the works of Roman lawyers and their legal documents, his favourite of which was Tacitus. The formation of new logic and methodology on the platform of the newly constituted humanistic sciences was Vico's lifelong project. The treatise *The New Science* is based on a legal approach to history and it became a springboard for all the modern concepts of the philosophy of history (however, Vico did not know the term "philosophy of history" and he did not use it either; it was introduced by Voltaire). He himself called his concept the "historical philology". (see: VICO, G.: *Základy nové vědy o společné přirozenosti národů*. p. 14)

When we trace the reasons why Vico used law as the base for his thinking about history, and mainly the basic law of nations, it becomes clear that for Vico law blends with society and is therefore a basic historical category of power.

However, his system of new science consists as an important moment for God as human society follows the instructions and develops on the grounds of its own inevitable causes, which result from human nature. Vico divides the historical development of mankind into three ages: the ages of divinities, heroes and civilization. Three kinds of nature correspond to the three ages. Three kinds of the natural rights of nations and three kinds of wisdom correspond to three kinds of nature. In the time of the divinities the law is in god's hands, in the time of heroes the law mingles with violence, which is mitigated by religion. In the time of civilization (humanity) the law is identified with human laws. The climax of history in Vico's works is connected with the last age, which is characterized by rules including equality, justice and law. These stand on completely developed human logic (this motif is elaborated by the philosophers of history in the Enlightenment). The political establishment that is dominant at Vico's peak of history is the monarchy, which is at first able to eliminate the inner and outer danger and conflicts in society. They are constantly rising. Vico in this place follows from the history of Rome where he sees the prototypes of historical process. Roman history shows the effort to establish some kind of an ideal "world community". The monarchy disappointed him by its failure to learn from Roman history. (see: LEMON, M.C.: *Philosophy of History*, pp. 135 – 137)

With regards to methodology, Vico follows on from the idea that rational nature is the same in all people. The idea of unity of human kind brought him to a comparative method, which he applied to all historic nations. Vico talks about eternal ideal history, where nations alternate, they gradually navigate their inception, progress, maturity decay and end (this almost biological approach to the historical development of nations, cultures or civilizations can be found later in the majority of authors). Vico also did not avoid the crucial question of the philosophy of history – when does history arise? The origination of history is, according to him, connected with the initial cultivation of humans. History arises when people start to be cultivated by religion from roughness and savagery. History then goes through the previously stated levels and is constantly in a cycle of *corco* and *ricorso*, of movement and countermovement (later O. Spengler and A. Toynbee adopted this conception). Vico's concepts cannot simply be deemed as finishing the old classic idea of the return of everything in a circle because Vico classifies the individual cycles into a spiral above each other so a certain progress in history cannot be ruled out.

5.9. The French Enlightenment

The philosophy of the 18th and 19th centuries is characterized by the fact that questions about the tendency of history, faith in progress and the almost unlimited possibilities of the human mind are coming to the fore.

Burghership starts to purposefully prepare for its rise to power by looking for concepts which would restrict a ruler's power. Freedom is a pillar in the consciousness of Enlightenment thinking. First it is the freedom of thought and belief and then the related freedom of speech and opinions. A tolerance issue (political and religious) is also connected with to these freedoms. This culminated in a claim for civil liberties. A new understanding of the responsibility of the state power resonated with society; power is controlled and in this situation the road is paved for revolution. The idea of progress becomes a uniting element of history and therefore the chronicle approach to history can be successfully overcome. Progress is perceived as the progress of the human spirit. It is not surprising then that the philosophy of history became a popular philosophical discipline during the Enlightenment. It is the result of the Enlightenment programme and efforts to capture the nature of social movement. The effort to articulate social-political-cultural events resulted in the creation of the philosophy of history. Representatives of the Enlightenment supposed that the historical process meant the increase of progress but unlike the medieval concepts they secularized the course and goal of history to a great extent when they transformed the Christian history of salvation into new events and human reason became an equivalent of God's Revelation. The philosophers of the Enlightenment realized that progress is conditioned by controlling social relations, which requires a suitably elaborated theory of society function and organization. The idea of progress was not a highly original "invention" of the thinkers in the Enlightenment time. It can be seen at least in the works of Francis Bacon and his programme motto "knowledge is power" or, for example, in the works of Jean Bodin, who in the 16th century was strongly against the opinions of gradual and inevitable degeneration of the human kind.

The possibility to perfect human kind results from an idea of progress that brings the contemporary optimism of the Enlightenment. The idealization of the past, which dominated in the Renaissance, is replaced by optimistic future ideals.

The history of human kind is no longer interpreted through the prism of the Scriptures, which determined the beginning and the end of human earthly history. God's community had been floating above an earthly community and had been showing the terminal goal of humans. History is compared with reason and vice versa where history and reason find possibilities for overcoming their limits.

5.10. Voltaire

François Marie Arouet Voltaire (1694 – 1778) was a thinker who was the first one to establish the term *philosophy of history*, (*la philosophie de l'historie*), in his treatise *Essay on the Customs and the Spirit of the Nations*. With the phrase "philosophy of history" Voltaire aptly described what Vico called "the new science". The philosophy of history is, according to French philosophers of the Enlightenment, neither the philosophy of law nor the philosophy of politics. When mentioning the controversial Voltaire, one must remark on the circumstances of the emergence of his interest in "philosophy of history". Voltaire shared a natural-legal stance on the organization society, taking inspiration from the theories of Lock and Montesquieu. As for the area of social philosophy he supported the reform of criminal law and humanization of punishment. Voltaire's approach to history is delimited in relation with both the theological understanding of history and the political and legal concepts of Machiavelli's and Vico's history. For Voltaire history means mainly a process of spiritual events which are driven by "discharges" of human spirit which are manifested in science, philosophy, politics and culture. The progress of human reason forms a starting point for cultural development and Voltaire seizes it by means of a gradual transition from barbarism to civilization. For him history means a process of continual change; everything is changing – the form of government, manners, customs, languages, etc. Voltaire's concept is extraordinary because his descriptions of historic events do not end in historiography, they go on, and they compare, e.g. European culture with Oriental. From this research, he drew the conclusion that everything connected with human nature is similar throughout the entire world and that which is connected with customs is different. A coincidence can be found only by chance. His philosophy of history reflects the historical development of a culture of individual nations. Voltaire held for some time the office of "court historian" during the reign of Louis XV and dealt with the issues of the philosophy of history in two more treatises: *The Age of Louis XIV* and *History of Charles XII*.

Reason was for him not only the main "tool" of historical reflection but also a proven weapon against fanaticism, superstition, ignorance and fear. A human is a human if he constantly longs for knowledge and this desire is conditioned by reason. Voltaire was strongly against the misinterpretation or forgery of history and he very critically refuted various utterances about historical events, which were not proven by their contemporaries, and marked them as fables. The human spirit, on its journey through history, is influenced by three factors: climate, government and religion. Knowing the causes of historical events is meaningful not only from the point of view of philosophical reflection on the past, but also because of the possibility to predict the future.

5.11. Condorcet

These ideas were naturally followed by Marie-Jean-Antoine-Nicolas Caritas, marquis de Condorcet (1743 – 1794) in his treatise *Sketch for a Historical Picture of the Progress of the Human Mind* claimed that *"...and analysis of the advance of the human mind and the development of its capacities yield the strongest grounds for believing that nature has set no limit to our hopes."* (CONDORCET, J. A.: *Náčrt historického obrazu pokroků lidského ducha.* p. 25) He understood progress as the deepening of educational level. He stressed, in the thoughts of the Enlightenment, the development of culture, morality, science and philosophy.

Condorcet determined, by means of many studies concerning historical materials, ten main historical epochs, which we can follow in history. Mankind has passed through nine of them; the last epoch follows after the victory of modern science and philosophy and is for now light years away. The first epoch of history is represented by a period when mankind lived a tribal way of life and made its living by hunting and fishing. The next epoch is represented by the change from the hunting way of life to agricultural life. The third one is characterized by a shift to a simple market economy. During this era, writes Condorcet, due to the advent of merchants and craftsmen communication among people improved vastly and this contributed to the invention of the alphabet. The fifth epoch was contingent on the conveniences of the ancient Greeks, however in contrast the sixth epoch was connected with the Romans and their culture. He describes this epoch as situated in the 11th century and dominated by the Crusades. In another historic epoch the Arabs, who conserved knowledge in the later Middle Ages after the invention of the printing press, were in the cultural foreground. (see: LEMON, M.C.: *Philosophy of History,* p. 190)

Despite all the failures, the above seven stages of history can be considered as "the progress of the human spirit". The eighth phase is accompanied by the invention of the printing press and the entire Renaissance, which laid the foundation for the ninth epoch – the Enlightenment and the scientific revolution that came with it.

The determinative milestones of human history were, according to Condorcet, emergence of writing, Greek science, the invention of the printing press and the birth of modern science. At the same time, he insisted that the natural relationships of social development can be comprehended (and therefore it is necessary to build social science, which Voltaire called "philosophy of history"). Condorcet's work includes the buds of a gradually emerging new social science, *sociology*. He unequivocally refuses wars, expansionism and inequality of races and nations; he clings to the idea of cooperation and tolerance. History as a gradual transition from a primitive human to a civilized one does not represent the decay of mankind although occasional descending lines and several crises in development can be found in history. It is necessary to add that although Condorcet insisted that historical natural relations and progress in the historical process is inevitable, but he in one breath refused the "religious superstitions" and "metaphysical absurdities".

5.12. Comte

The French Enlightenment with its optimistic tendencies quite naturally culminated in one of the most influential movements of postclassical philosophy – positivism. Positivism is usually divided into three phases but the first one affected the issues of philosophy of history most significantly. This phase is called the classical phase and A. Comte, J.S. Mill, H. Spencer and others were some of its key figures.

Auguste Comte (1798-1857) oriented his works to the constitution of science, which would stand on positive principles in opposition to theological and metaphysical speculation. His thinking was influenced by the traditions of Enlightenment and its concepts of social progress. He was strongly influenced by Turgot (historic stages) and by Condorcet (continuity of history). Comte was convinced that the time of positive philosophy had come, which is grounded in the facts and permanent relations between them and laws. (see: ZIGO, M.: *August Comte. In: Malá antológia z diel filozofov II., p. 14*) Philosophy principally does not say more about the world than science. Is philosophy then legitimate? Comte finds its function in the creation of the classification of science and in the answers to questions, such as the philosophical base: what is science? What is the purpose of science? He answers the first question with the statement that it is finding facts and their permanent relationships. The second question is dealt with under the influence of F. Bacon – science enables us to foresee and subsequently to control nature. (see: ZIGO, M.: *August Comte. In: Malá antológia z diel filozofov II.*, p. 14)

Comte analysed the development of human reason in his treatise *The Course in Positive Philosophy* in three stages: theological, metaphysical and positive. In the theological stage human reason focuses on "... *seeking the essential nature of beings, the first and final causes ... —in short, Absolute knowledge,—supposes all phenomena to be produced by the immediate action of supernatural beings."* (COMTE, A.: *Kurz pozitívnej filozofie*. In: *Malá antológia z diel filozofov II.* p. 16).

According to Comte, in the metaphysical stage supernatural factors are replaced by abstract forces or substances. In the positive stage the human spirit is aware of the fact that absolute knowledge cannot be acquired, *"...has given over the vain search after Absolute notions, the origin and destination of the universe, and the coituses of phenomena, and applies itself to the study of their laws, — that is, their invariable relations of succession and resemblance."* (COMTE, A.: *Kurz pozitívnej filozofie.* In: *Malá antológia z diel filozofov II.* p. 16)

The speculative philosophy of history transformed sociology, which Comte founded (however, indications of this science can be already seen in Condorcet's works). Together with positivism, scientism started to dominate in philosophy and ended the philosophy of history (most visibly in Popper.)

5.13. The German Enlightenment and History

Without exaggeration we can say that if the questions of philosophy of history in the French Enlightenment were extraordinarily popular, then late 18th and early 19th century German philosophy elevated them to the par excellence of philosophical problems. We can find an idea of the progress and privileged position of reason in history in the concepts of the German authors of this period. As presented by professor Marcelli, reason and history, or more precisely the requirement of a rational unity and reality of historical plurality, were also present in the previous periods. The Enlightenment is peculiar because reason does not need nature any more, which offered the possibility to *"...characterize the typical features of the rational approach on the background of its regularity, randomness and unrestrainedness."* (MARCELLI, M.: *Filozofi v meste.p. 102*) Both the refusal and acceptance of the results of historical changes belong to the manifestations of reason. On the other hand, history can, despite its random nature, bring a reasonable result. (see: MARCELLI, M.: *Filozofi v meste.* p. 103)

5.14. Herder

Johann Gottfried von Herder (1744 – 1803) created a concept, which is termed *naturalistic historicism* since his interpretation of history and social development connects the development of nature with the development of society. Herder mainly engaged with history in his work *Ideas for the Philosophy of the History of Humanity*. From the outset of *"Development of Humanity"* he presents the reasons for his interest in philosophy: *"...when everything in the world has its philosophy and science, what concerns us the most should have it too and thus the history of the mankind."* (HERDER, J.G.: *Vývoj lidskosti.* p. 6)

For Herder, who was strongly influenced by B. Spinoza, history is the continuation of cosmologic development and nature is personified in his concept: *"...nature is not an individual being but God is in all his works everything... who sees the word "nature" in all the treatises of our century as meaningless and inferior should replace it with the almighty power, goodness and wisdom...*" (HERDER, J.G.: *Vývoj lidskosti.* p. 9) According to Herder, the base of history is composed of the history of the solar system, the Earth, the plant kingdom and the animal kingdom. Naturalism can clearly be felt in such an approach, which brings an idea of causality to the thinking about history. Herder weakens the theological approach by means of naturalism. History is, in his opinion, a science about what really exists and not about what *could* exist or be realized in the name of fate or providence. History should be then interpreted as a *determined* sequence of causes and effects.

Humans emerged in history as a natural part (a product) of nature and therefore the historical laws of mankind are analogous with the history of nature. The idea of progress in Herder's concept understood as a gradual formation of humanity, which is executed in the course of historical progress through the genius of nations (this is the reason why the philosophy of history is usually defined as the philosophy of the history of humanity) Mankind is, during the progress of history, passing through several cultural stages and changes where the basic platform of progress consists of reason and justice. Three laws affecting this can be, in Herder's opinion, seen in history – the first law determines nations as a history formatting subject and it informs the importance of their mutual influence; the second law claims that good and evil have their place in history and as a result they contribute to human development. The third and main law at the same time says: *"It happens everywhere on the Earth what can happen, according to position and needs of the given place, partly according to circumstances and period causes, partly according to inborn or cultivated nature of nations."* (HERDER, J.G.: *Vývoj lidskosti.p.223*) The history of mankind is formed by the nations (empires) that alternate at the head of the human race according to when they fulfil their task in the historic development of humanity. A nation which fulfils its historic role, makes place for another nation and so on *"a nation follows a nation, an empire follows an empire and majority of them have (already) disappeared from the Earth except for names and ... memorials."* (HERDER, J.G.: *Vývoj lidskosti.p.223*) Each nation has its place and time and is characterized by a specific culture, art, moral strength and so on. The function of historical process is not a mechanical alternation of the individual national cultures but, as Herder's first law says, their mutual influence. A nation as a subject of history cannot be identified with the state at all. A nation is "a natural organism" while the state is an artificial product; states vanish but nations persist. (HERDER, J.G.: *Vývoj lidskosti.* p. 244)

Herder's opinions on the history of the Slavs are also a part of his work. The Slavs are defined as one nation, or more precisely one ethnic community, which is characterized by a lot of residents and a huge area, which they inhabit. The Slavs have in Herder's eyes a great potential for spiritual strength and the prerequisites for cultural-artistic production, ability to learn and to progress. They are also known for their diligence (land cultivation, crop growing, farming, craftsmanship and the like). Their nature is, according to Herder, peaceful, warm-hearted, kind, respectful, hospitable, unselfish, patient and obedient. It follows from this characteristic that the Slavs should be given a specific position in history: *"The wheel of time is turning unstoppably and because these (Slavic) nations inhabit primarily the most beautiful parts of Europe... neither here is it conceivable in other way that the European laws will have to support the silent diligence and peaceful mutual enrichment of the nations instead of a fighting spirit and so also these deeply sunk and in former times hardworking nations will wake up from their long sleep and they will then free themselves from the slave chains, they will use their beautiful regions from the Adriatic sea to the Carpathian Mountains and from the Danube to the Vltava River as their property and they will celebrate their old holidays of peaceful diligence and work in their freed villages."* (HERDER, J.G.: *Vývoj lidskosti.p.332*) It is indisputable, that Herder's "vision" contributed to the formation and reflection of historic national consciousness of many Slavic nations (he influenced also Kollár, Štúr and others).

Let us stop at the question how we, according to Herder, actually move towards humanity. It is mechanical lifelong "training" where we learn from the traditions and failures of the past. History is dependent on the rules of justice and injustice or on law and lawlessness. Herder gives an example from the history of social philosophy: Herder disagrees principally with *The Prince* by Machiavelli because it is not possible to consider mankind to be a line, which can be arbitrarily shortened or elongated. Herder says that there is no such form of government that could be applied to all nations in the same way.

Herder writes that the development of education and gradual "humanization" of a human started in Asia and spread out from there. The emergence of language and writing played a great role in this emergence. The historic development had an upward tendency due to key nations such as the Oriental and Egyptian nations, the nations of Persia, Greece, Rome and later the European nations. The "nation" topic, which was opened by Herder, comes into play later thanks to Nietzsche, Spengler and others.

5.15. Kant and his Contribution to History

Immanuel Kant (1724 – 1804) dealt with the issues of history mainly in his so-called small treatises. He interpreted history in the most concentrated way in the work *Idea for a Universal History with a Cosmopolitan Purpose*.

In this work we can find an overlap of Kant's opinions from both the pre-critical and critical period. A human is, according to Kant, an inhabitant of two empires: an empire of nature (inevitability) and an empire of freedom.

In his opinion, over the course of history a human's activity is realized on the basis of nature: *"...human deeds are yet determined, like any other natural occurrences, by the general natural laws..."* (KANT, I.: *Idey k všeobecným dejinám v svetoobčianskom zmysle.* In: KANT, I.: *K večnému mieru.* p.57), so we can discover in them a certain regularity. Even if it is not obvious at first sight, this regularity is present in all actions in nature. A regular process can be found in history in the same way as in the uninterrupted functions of plants, river flows, movement of animals and other creations of nature. (see: KANT, I.: *Idey k všeobecným dejinám v svetoobčianskom zmysle.* In: KANT, I.: *K večnému mieru.* p. 57)

With regard to Kant's work and his way of arguing, it is not surprising that he tried to interpret history through reason. A human started to predict the future from the historical process and because of reason he started to have certain expectations for the future. He started to be aware of the fact that nature can be used to his advantage. When he understood for the first time that nature did not give fur to a sheep but to him to wear it, a human realized that he himself is the goal of nature.

This was the very reason that did not allow a human to come back to the state *"...of brutality and naivety from which it pulled him out... "*. (KANT, I.: *Idey k všeobecným dejinám v svetoobčianskom zmysle.* In: KANT, I.: *K večnému mieru.* p. 57) When Kant contemplates history, he deals with human kind and not with an individual since the life of an individual is too short for using all their natural talents which are, according to him, one of the goals of history. An individual human life is too short to fulfil the possibilities of direction towards progress. Mankind as a whole gradually comes to the development of all talents thanks to *antagonism of individuals in the society.* *"Antagonism is understood as an unsociable sociability of people i.e. their tendency to enter the society connected with loathing, which is constantly putting the society in danger of dividing."* (KANT, I.: *Idey k všeobecným dejinám v svetoobčianskom zmysle.* In: KANT, I.: *K večnému mieru.* p. 61) On one hand, a human tends to unite and conform, but on the other he also desires to excel in society and separate himself from it ("this internal fight" was elaborated by F. Fukuyama two centuries later in the form of a dichotomy of isothymia and magalothymia).

Kant claims that the aim of history is the creation of a general civil society, which will be ruled by law. He comprehends history as a realization of a hidden intention of nature and the creation of a political establishment, which will be *"... a perfect state establishment as a single status in which the nature can fully develop all its talents in the mankind."* (KANT, I.: *Idey k všeobecným dejinám v svetoobčianskom zmysle.* In: KANT, I.: *K večnému mieru.* p. 68)

Kant considers war to be the biggest evil in the historical process or more precisely mainly continual armament for the next war and since huge financial and social means are necessary for this, morality declines and freedom is violated. Mankind has to reach a stage when wars are no longer beneficial and worldwide peace is established.

5.16. Hegel

Georg Wilhelm Friedrich Hegel (1770 – 1831) is a key person due to his contribution to the philosophy of history. He categorized the philosophy of history into his philosophical system and dedicated a separate treatise *Philosophy of History* of the same name to it, which was published in 1837.

He distinguishes three kinds of history in the philosophy of history: original, reflecting and philosophical history.

The first type, original history, is based on Herodotus and Thucydides. This history is not extensive and it concerns a description of events, which the author experienced himself, or more precisely, which he learnt from other people. There is a lack of reflections, reflection essays, because the author observes the described events from the present viewpoint without any view removed in time. The second type is reflecting history. This kind of interpretation differs from original history because it extends beyond the present. He distinguishes several types within this interpretation. The first one deals with a history interpretation of one country. Since the described periods are mostly longer some events are fading out or are left out. This kind of reflecting history is called *general history writing*. Another type is the *pragmatic approach to history* when the past is reflected and incorporated into the present. The third and last type of reflecting history is a *critical* one. It is not a case of writing the history itself but an assessment of interpretation of history, which means the evaluation of whether the facts are true, if the statements are true, trustworthy and following one after another. This kind of history is a transition to the last type of history – the philosophical history of the world. Philosophy of history is, in this interpretation, a branch of history. According to Hegel, the philosophy brings an idea that reason controls the world and so the history of the world will be in progress under the strict supervision of reason which is a basic prerequisite of history itself. In Hegel's opinion, reason is *"...as well as Infinite Power; its own Infinite Material underlying all the natural and spiritual life which it originates, as also the Infinite Form — that which sets this Material in motion."* (HEGEL, G. W. F.: *Filozofia dejín*. p. 17)

Hegel restricts history to the development of reason in the life of a state so his concept deals mainly with political history. Hegel openly despised those who looked for the meaning of history and life in happiness: *"The History of the World is not the theatre of happiness. Periods of happiness are blank pages in it, for they are periods of harmony — periods when the antithesis is in abeyance."* (HEGEL, G. W. F.: *Filozofia dejín*. p. 30) He believes that everything in history happens in a sensible way: *"The reason controls the world so the History of the World is in progress in a reasonable way."* (HEGEL, G. W. F.: *Filozofia dejín*. p. 30) History is then a development of a deeper logic by which all nations are overpowered but the great historic personalities – they are only its unconscious tool, a "will of the world spirit". The meaning in history does not acquire individuality (similarly to Kant's belief) but its incorporation into transpersonal historical forces and processes. Individuals do not affect history but the world spirit does by means of individuals. It follows that personal energy or talent do not make the great personalities what they are (mainly when we, according to Hegel, consider that the world spirit often uses weak individuals for its purposes) but the reality that historic essentiality, "the spirit of the age", is personalized in them. These so-called world-historic personalities are often controlled by passions: *"without passion nothing great would be done in the world."* (HEGEL, G. W. F.: *Filozofia dejín*. p. 30), and they threw themselves thoughtlessly into one purpose. They represent heroes for Hegel because their instinct was able to do something that was right and essential for history. Everything in his concept of the philosophy of history is subordinate to the absolute *Spirit*. World history is a stage in the development of the spirit and it consists of the consciousness of freedom: *"This result it is, at which the process of the World's History has been continually aiming; and to which the sacrifices that have ever and anon been laid on the vast altar of the earth"* (HEGEL, G. W. F.: *Filozofia dejín*. p. 26)

History seemed to be the history of a non-living substance in a certain period of time, whereas living organisms came on stage later. The history of the spirit begins with the emergence of a human. It does not mean that the spirit had not existed before humans emerged; it had been here since the creation of the world, however, only with the emergence of humans did it start to gain self-awareness. According to Hegel, historic development developed *linearly* in four epochs: *Oriental, Greek, Roman and Graeco-Christian*. These historic periods correspond to four stages of human life – childhood, youth, adulthood and old age. A historic cradle of social inequality and injustice is, according to Hegel, the Ancient East. It began to manifest in China at first in the form of patriarchal despotism, then in India in the caste system, which is based on the primitive distribution of labour and tribal exogamy. In Persia and Egypt the military-theocratic despotism was dominant. The East, in Hegel's opinion, reached its climax in Persian culture and decline can be seen in Egypt, which Hegel considers to be some kind of connecting link between The East and the Greco-Roman world. The Greeks and their epoch are characterized as a period of aesthetics, which is proven by Greek myths, symbols and allegories. The world of the Greeks was based on family love and the fight against robbery unlike the Romans, who Hegel views much more critically; acts of violence, banditry (the establishment of Rome itself was violent), wildness are the side effects of the Romans. According to Hegel, the Germanic world (nations of the Western Europe) is the highest stage of history. A task of this epoch is to develop the Christian principle (Hegel identified specifically with Protestantism) – freedom for all people. Hegel did not consider the beginnings of the Germanic-Christian culture to be particularly important as he was more interested in the Middle Ages, which he also regarded very critically. The medieval Christian consciousness is seen as split between "this" and "that" world. He also evaluates negatively the politicized medieval church, the decline of the clergy and the feudal system in the social sphere, which is, according to him, a worldly realization of Christianity.

The most significant period in Hegel's works is the modern age, which is grounded on two pillars – the first one is reformation, which is a symbol of 'real' Christianity and brings freedom, the second pillar of the modern age is the French Revolution, which executed a world-historic idea that freedom should be a generally applicable law.

We can then conclude that, for Hegel the nations of the Oriental world did not reflect themselves in the historical process, they were static. Their ahistoricity and static character manifest themselves in an undeveloped individual and in the inability to think freely and rationally. Only *on eperson* (ruler) is free in the Orient. Not even Greek culture represents free individuality even though *polis* starts to form the elements of individual thinking and decision making of the citizens. A citizen – community – law relation emerges. Hegel defines the culture of the Roman Empire as an attempt to return to Oriental despotism although the Romans were already enriched with the ability to think individually, which they acquired from the Greeks. Hegel finds the following most important historic events in the Germanic world: migration of peoples, the reign of Charles IV, crusades, art and science as a decline of the Middle Ages, the modern age with the reformation movement and the Enlightenment with revolution. Hegel does not consider the reformation only as a change in the perfecting of religion but, rather as a way to realize real freedom. An exemplary embodiment of the realization of freedom was paradoxically contemporary Prussia.

Let us go back to the basic thesis of Hegel's entire philosophy of history – history is a development of the spirit in time. It is the case of a gradual process of spreading the idea of freedom. History is a perpetual penetration of ideas to freedom and the citizens' consciousness. *State* is the objectification of freedom. Nations, which did not create a state, do not belong to history and they are therefore ahistoric (such as the Slavs).

After Hegel's death a fight for his philosophical heritage erupted for obvious reasons, opinions on history are no exception. A. Schopenhauer, who disapproved of the idea of the development of history and its diversity, categorically opposed his concepts. F. Nietzsche adopted a similar attitude to Hegel's philosophy of history and he also refused the linear concept of history. S. Kierkegaard did not spare the criticism either. According to him, Hegel relativizes good and evil and reduces an individual to a historical process of spirit development. K. Marx was inspired by Hegel's philosophy of history for a long time but eventually disassociated with it, denied Hegel's concepts and "turned him head over heels". In the twentieth century A. Kojéve, K.R. Poppert and F. Fukuyama (among others) revived Hegel's philosophy of history.

5.17. Nietzsche and History

Friedrich Wilhelm Nietzsche (1844 – 1900) contributed to the discussion about the philosophy of history in his voluntaristic first philosophical work *The Birth of Tragedy* where he outlined original and provocative views on history. In this treatise he deals with ancient drama to which he attributes two forms – Apollonian and Dionysian. One side of the ancient drama is rationality, moderation, desire for perfection (Apollonian principle) and the second, dark side is the Dionysian principle of an even orgiastic intoxication with life, fullness of experiences, and instinctual indulgence of every moment.

The Apollonian and Dionysian principles compete with each other in all areas of life – the Apollonian approach is an obstinate desire for perfection – Apollo the God himself acts as the guardian of individuality; those who worship him are armed with rationality. (NIETZSCHE, F.: *Zrození tragedie.* p. 13) The devotees of Dionysus forget their individuality and although they see themselves as a passing phenomenon it participates in authentic life and being: *"Everything present is just and unjust and equally justified in both."* (NIETZSCHE, F.: *Zrození tragedie.* p. 36) According to Nietzsche, the Dionysian principle with its "fullness of instincts" and nodding to life is primary. Human fate is an effort to harmonize both of the elements, the revolt and nodding. In his concept Nietzsche declines the Christian eschatological idea of history and he sympathises more with an elaborated concept of the *eternal return.* It is possible to say unequivocally that Nietzsche surprised all with a newly elaborated idea of the *eternal return* since he presented at the time when most of the authors identify the linear understanding of the historical process (cyclical approach appears very rarely in this time, the last time it was mentioned was by Vico).

Nietzsche's eternal return does not take place in the background of numb silence of the archaic time. History is for mankind an opportunity to celebrate life and it is also an unending fight between the Apollonian element and the Dionysian one in a form of the reassessment of values. In Nietzsche's opinion, if one principle takes power for a long time it has terrifying consequences for history: the balance in history is violated. It happens often in history – sometimes an epoch emphasizing reasonableness, concentration on the universal interpretation of the world and on the firm form of the interpretation of reality is dominant and at another time the opposite principle wins – barbarism, disappearance of respect for wisdom and religion. This time is, according to Nietzsche, *a circle* which means "a process" without the beginning and end.

Nietzsche manifested his ideas about time and history in the treatises *Untimely Meditations, Thus spoke Zarathustra* and *Beyond Good and Evil.* In *Untimely Meditations* he emphasizes that we need history but in a form other than a mindless and shapeless science. "... *their desire is rather to arouse their time to life in order to live on themselves in this life.*" (NIETZSCHE, F.: *Nečasové úvahy I.* p. 83)

According to Nietzsche, history should serve life; this is its main function. He criticises his age, which is proud of historic education even of some kind of historic fever. Unlike the humans animals live ahistorically. They do not know what the past, present and future is. But the human lives *historically*, he is constantly burdened with the past, which bends him down to the ground and does not allow him to move. In Nietzsche's opinion, a look at a herd, peacefully grazing, not burdened with time or at a child, who is too little to deny anything and lives in blissful ignorance can move us.

An innocent child's play will end one day and the child will understand the word "was", the word which brings sorrows. An individual, a nation and even an entire culture needs the ahistorical and the historical in moderation. Nietzsche mentions the Ancient Greeks, who were in a similar danger as we are now – in danger of death in the flood of the past. But the Greeks were able to overcome the danger of death by a Delphian statement; they recollected themselves, their real needs and they left the apparent needs to die. Nietzsche thinks that this is a challenge for each of us: *"culture is some kind of life decoration."* (NIETZSCHE, F.: *Nečasové úvahy I.* p. 165) The concept of culture will open up for us as a concept of a new and improved nature, without pretence and static convention. The real culture is, as a matter of fat, a harmony between life, thinking and wanting. Nietzsche understands the world where history goes on as a monstrous power, which is not getting stronger or weaker; it is only changing in the historical process. History is driven by an ardent will to live, which makes life restore itself. The most important manifestation of will is the will for power, which is in Nietzsche's case interpreted as a positive value. In history mankind has to reassess all the values which have been strengthened so far by the Jewish-Christian tradition. A space will be gradually created so that the will for power will be able to culminate in an *overman*, who can be seen as some kind of a result of the entire evolution process of the mankind. But he is not a result of a mechanical natural process, it is rather a case of human activity product: „*The overman is the meaning of the earth.*" (NIETZSCHE, F.: *Tak vravel Zarathustra*. p. 9) Nietzsche also appeals to people not to yield to magic of transcendence. Zarathustra calls:" *I appeal to you, my brothers, remain true to the earth, and do not believe those who speak to you of otherworldly hopes!*" (NIETZSCHE, F.: *Tak vravel Zarathustra*.p. 9) The last man for Nietzsche is a follower of so-called slave morality the declaration of which is Christianity – the religion of the weak. This man deserves only contempt although it is difficult to remove him from the world: "*His race is as ineradicable as the flea; the last man lives longest.*" (NIETZSCHE, F.: *Tak vravel Zarathustra*. p. 13)

The overman should be the one who comes after the last man and will be his personalization of so-called aristocratic morality. *"I picked up from the path the word "overman," and that man is something that must be surpassed."* (NIETZSCHE, F.: *Tak vravel Zarathustra*. p. 10)

The overman should be a superior kind of a man who fights with the slave morality. Nietzsche accuses Christians that they have made up false values like mercy, virtues, brotherly love and help, humbleness and the like. They endanger the strong ones – they teach them to be ashamed of their strength and health. Zarathustra says in connection with equality: *"For thus speaks justice to me: "Men are not equal."* (NIETZSCHE, F.: *Tak vravel Zarathustra*. p. 105) It follows from the above that humanism, which was proclaimed by the representatives of the Enlightenment, completes, for Nietzsche, the individual way and there can be no question of democracy which is based on equality in connection with his conception of philosophy of history.

5.18. Spengler

Oswald Spengler's (1880 – 1936) interpretation of history cannot be overlooked in our overview of the individual concepts of philosophical history. This German thinker made his mark in the history of thinking due to his pessimistic vision of history, which was delineated in two large treatises: *The Decline of the West* and *Man and Technics*. As a philosopher he gave an impression of an eclectic: he connected Bergson's intuitivism and his philosophy of life with Schopenhauer's impersonal will, Nietzsche's irrationalism, Kant's theory of knowledge with the language of the Romanticists. He added to this broad gamut of opinions and methods an assumption that the individual cultures of mankind (which he examined in detail) are soulful and their mental uniqueness creates all the demonstrations in the spiritual area – philosophy, religion, art, law and politics so we can even feel here an affinity to the Romanticists and their teachings about the nation spirit. Spengler based the main grounds of his philosophy on Bergsonian dualism – he put the world of things, which yields to causality, in opposition to the world of history with constant action and change, which is not controlled by causality and laws. Bergson's influence can be seen not only in the determination of dual opposition but also in the characterization of the "world of history" as the world of change, actions, instability, vitality, new formation. It is not law, number and logic that is important in the historical reality but the *shape*. This is a reference to Goethe's "ideal form", which is entirely historical and it cannot be seized by means of analytical way of thinking. (see: THURNHER, RÖD, SCHMIDINGER:*Filosofie 19. a 20. století.* p. 102)

He named the examination of historical shapes "morphology of history" which again refers to Goethe. According to Spengler, the task of contemporary civilization became to work out the morphology of the world history in opposition to the morphology of nature, which had been dominating history so far: *"The world-as-history, conceived, viewed and given form from out of its opposite the world-as-nature – here is a new aspect of human existence on this earth. As yet, in spite of its immense significance, both practical and theoretical, this aspect has not been realized, still less presented."* (SPENGLER, O.: *Zánik Západu. Obrysy morfológie svetových dějin.* p. 19) In Spengler's opinion, there is still not any theoretically clear art of historic observance and everything that is usually described this way draws its methods solely from the area of physics: *"...and thus we imagine ourselves to be carrying on historical research when we are really following out objective connexions of cause and effect. It is a remarkable fact that the old-fashioned philosophy never imagined even the possibility of there being any other relation than this between the conscious human understanding and the world outside."* (SPENGLER, O.: *Zánik Západu. Obrysy morfológie svetových dějin.* p. 20)

Here Spengler spares his criticism of I. Kant who, in his opinion, only considered nature as an object of reason's activity while determining the formal rules of knowledge. Knowledge, for Kant, is mathematical knowledge. Spengler also criticizes A. Schopenhauer who speaks *"...contemptuously of history."* (SPENGLER, O.: *Zánik Západu. Obrysy morfológie svetových dějin.* p. 20) According to Spengler, it is possible to deduce the "soul" from cultural forms and the soul is the base of each culture. This teaching of his results in pan-symbolism and in the idea that life, which possesses existence even though it has not been fully awakened, connects the whole in an all-embracing way so that it is possible to grasp the whole from the individual. Spengler understands cultures as organisms of a higher kind, which have not only a soul but they can be born, grow, mature, get old and die the same way as plants or animals. Culture is a manifestation of the creative mind, as soon as it dies and stops creating it changes into a "civilization."

Spengler distinguishes eight high cultures in history – *Chinese, Indian, Babylonian, Egyptian, Ancient, Mexican, Russian* and *Western* (Faustian). These cultures need to be perceived as individual wholes or, rather, *forms*, they are mutually exclusive, and they don't grow one from another. Each culture has in all its manifestations certain particularities, characteristics, which represent the idea of a thinking human. By way of the introduction of *The Decline of the West*, Spengler asks the question if *"there is a logic of history. Is there, beyond all the casual and incalculable elements of the separate events, something that we may call a metaphysical structure of historic humanity, something that is essentially independent of the outward forms – social, spiritual and political- which we see so clearly?"* (SPENGLER, O.: *Zánik Západu. Obrysy morfológie světových dějin*. p. 17) In Spengler's opinion, it is not possible to causally deduce where the new culture emerges and what kind of manifestations it will have just as it is impossible to "calculate" the birth of a genius in history. In his opinion, mathematics and analogy is the best method for the understanding of living forms.

It means that we cannot understand history by searching for the causal non-binding nature of forms but by their mutual comparison. The beginnings of culture emerge when a castle with ruling nobility rises up above the agricultural land and a church with Church rule. In the following stage a town is built as an opposite of a village, which is gradually acquiring more and more significance; art and particularly science is being developed. Spengler says that as the towns are growing culture is transitioned into the civilization stage. "Common people" come into play and they promote their ideologies – materialism and socialism. Culture is dying.

Spengler offered one of the most pessimistic concepts in the sphere of the philosophy of history. According to him, all optimistic visions (the Marxist communist paradise, or the scientific shift of mankind towards the post-industrial society of overabundance) need to be included in anecdotes – the human world is not ruled by reason and morality but by blind will. Spengler, as a historical fatalist, does not believe that the decline of the West can be turned around.

5.19. Jaspers

Karl Theodor Jaspers (1883 – 1969) tried to find in his philosophy of history universal criteria of the spiritual history of the world, i.e. criteria that would not be limited to the European tradition. He reflected on the history of philosophy, events of the First and Second World War, contemporary science, politics on a platform of philosophy of existence. He dealt with history mainly in the works *Small School of Philosophical Thought, Way to Wisdom, The Spiritual Situation of Time*.

Jaspers offers the following empirical picture of history: *"Prehistory without literature has existed ten thousands of years and maybe more. Documented history started approximately ten thousand years ago. First highly developed cultures in Mesopotamia, Egypt, India and China arose in the area which is on a map pictured as a narrow stripe interspaced with deserts between the Atlantic and Pacific Ocean. In the period between 800 to 200 BC spiritual events emerged independently from each other in China, India, Iran, Palestine and Greece (not in Mesopotamia and Egypt), which were the base for the consciousness, which we know today."* (JASPERS, K.: *Malá škola filozofického myslenia.* p. 26) According to Jaspers, the basic philosophical and religious questions were created at that time. He calls this period *on the axis of world history* (see: JASPERS, K.: *Malá škola filozofického myslenia.* p. 26) and deduces three basic development lines from it, which progressed in parallel – one of them in China, another in India and the third in the West. Also a human as we know him today emerged in the given period (cca. → 800 – 200 BC) and many important events happened – Confucius and Lao – c' in China, Upanishad was created in India, Buddha lived there, Zarathustra was active in Iran, prophets from Elijah to Deutero-Isaiah lived in Palestine, Homer, Parmenides, Heraclitus, Plato and Archimedes lived in Greece. *"All the vast development of which these names are a mere intimation took place in these few centuries, independently and almost simultaneously in China, India, and the West."* (Jaspers, K.: Úvod do filosofie) Jaspers also thinks that to approximately 1400 the technical means, a way of work and life forms in general were very similar in the three big cultures mentioned. Rationalization began as a direct result of technology, but only in Europe, in all areas – *"... a systematically inventing and continuously advancing technology."* (JASPERS, K.: *Malá škola filozofického myslenia*, p. 27) The control of nature, goods production, air and sea transport, which connected the entire Earth, became a historic revolution. Mankind was overwhelmed by a technical era, which became, according to Jaspers, grounds for historical process. It is necessary to distinguish the history of mankind from the history of nature, as could be seen with other authors. Our history is not the history of nature, it is not a continuation of the universe; it is of a completely different character. History of nature is a perpetual continuation of the same in the course of millions of years; history of mankind is incomparably shorter. It is related to traditions, conscious memories, and deeds. History in its entirety is unknown to man: *"Science about history is limited by the fact that we do not know the history in its wholeness as one meaningful whole. Empirical science about history encounters a coincidence all the time."* (JASPERS, K.: *Malá škola filozofického myslenia.* p. 30) The future course of history is also unknown to us. Jaspers does not sympathise with the pessimistic vision, in which the historic process is interpreted in actions which lead to the self-destruction of mankind. Love, the beauty of the works created by man, the entire world of norms and the greatness of man has to indicate something that extends beyond the end. Despite the dark times and situations, in which Jaspers' philosophy was created, there are some marks of optimism left in his concepts. Philosophers must not devote themselves to pessimistic visions and sinister prophecies. Historical observation (either *philosophical* or *empirical*) satisfies not only our knowledge. Its real mission is to arouse responsibility to the effect that we have to always make a decision what to follow, what to refuse and how to act. Jaspers suggests that we should be led by the high standards of our predecessors, which we adopt. *"We have to take over the commitments of our predecessors because we are responsible for them. We cannot escape from our origin."* (JASPERS, K.: *Malá škola filozofického myslenia.* p. 34)

It follows that we can experience freedom only when planning the future. Jaspers has no illusions about faith and life forms, which connect mankind, having one and only one meaning. However, there is something universal and particularly a political peace fellowship – Jaspers defines here an important role for philosophy and it is *"...remind that the future is opened and every beautiful arrangement of the human matters is limited..."* (JASPERS, K.: *Malá škola filozofického myslenia.* p. 34) These words express the refusal of any totalitarian or utopian concepts (e.g. K.R. Popper calls this approach historicism and he means *"the approach to social sciences, which says that their main goal is historic prediction and this goal can be reached by revelation of rhythms or formulas, laws or trends, which are hiding in the background of the historical process."* For more information on his understanding of historicism see POPPER, K.R.: Bída historicismu. Praha : OIKOYMENH, 1994.) History does not represent captivity for us; it should rather be understood as a "place" where we with our existence can come to what it really is. According to Jaspers, to emerge from history means to enter nothingness, thus history should not be ignored or refused.

Points of Reflection:

Which of the mentioned philosophic approaches to history is in your opinion the most acceptable? Why? What do you consider to be the driven forces of history? Finally: does history have meaning? How would you characterize the terms *the meaning* and *significance* of history?

Recommended literature:

LEMON, M.C.: *Philosophy of History*, London: Routledge, 2003.
POPPER, K.R.: *The Poverty of Historicism.* Routledge Classics, 2002.
SPENGLER, O.: *The Decline of the west.* Oxford University Press US, 1991.

6. Philosophy and Science

Since its inception, philosophy has been coexisted cosily with science (at that time with protoscience). The first philosophers did not contemplate the infinity, as Patočka says, but they existed at the same time the co-founders of science. (see: Patočka, J.: *Vznik filosofie*, p. 114)

The theoretical approach to the world mediated through wonder and doubts was gradually dividing and separating from philosophy. The limits of questions, which can be answered unequivocally, started to be uncovered and then emerged the questions that still cannot be answered unequivocally even today. The first ones were assumed by science and the second ones by philosophy. What is the difference between them? *"... science is characterized by the fact that it is based on canon of relatively firmly defined starting points, methods and procedures, which it comes from, with the help of which it chooses questions to be answered and with the help of which it searches for the answers to these questions."* (Peregrin, J.: Filosofie pro normální lidi, p. 16). Scientific knowledge has, unlike philosophical knowledge, ascending and cumulative character. Since the time of Hippocrates we have clearly and definitively moved forward in medicine but the questions that nagged at Plato have still not been answered satisfactorily and we have not progressed beyond Plato's original responses. Philosophy does not present any generally applicable results, unlike the way science fundamentally does for nature. Science in its most self-evident form improves the quality of our lives: we have longer and more effective drugs for a great number of diseases, we use cars, planes, and spacecraft to shorten previously inconceivable distances, we invented telephones, computers, the internet, robots, which exercise many activities instead of us. We are discovering the universe, the macro universe as well as the micro world. Scientific results are provide tangible results, something which cannot be said (generally speaking) for philosophical results. But a more in depth examination will reveal that philosophy, as delineated in the previous chapters, provides vital opportunities for critical thinking and developing new approaches to the world around us in a constant effort to know the truth, something which functions as an irreplaceable driving force of our culture.

Points of Reflection:

Try finding the philosophers in literature who were scientists as well? How did they perceive the border between philosophy and science?

Recommended literature:

BUNGE, M.: Critical Approaches to Science and Philosophy.
COLODNY, R.G.: Frontiers of Science and Philosophy. University of
   Pittsburgh, 1963.

Instead of Conclusion

In the presented textbook we tried outlining the basic topics of philosophy, starting from the term philosophy itself. We delineated it in a broader way in the context of culture, myth and science. We introduced thematic groups and questions of the individual philosophical disciplines and mapped the approaches of the individual authors of history of philosophy to the topic of history. An attentive reader can find the reflection essays and recommended literature at the conclusion of each chapter. It is advisable to study this extra information carefully. Without philosophical texts your study will remain shallow and *non-philosophical*. Philosophy does not represent only a sum of critical thinking, love for truth, knowledge, wisdom but also honesty. Read plenty and read dutifully if you plan on becoming model students of philosophy – or better yet model philosophers!

Bibliography

ANZENBACHER, A.: Úvod do filozofie, 1990, Praha: SPN.
ARISTOTELES, Metafyzika, 2003, Praha: Rezek.
BERĎAJEV, N.A.: Smysl dějin., 1995, Praha: OIKOYMENH.
BOËTHIUS, A. M. S.: *Filosofie utěšitelka*.1995, Olomouc: Votobia.
BOËTHIUS, A. M. S.: Filosofie utěšitelkou. In: Boëthius. Poslední Říman. 1982, Praha: Vyšehrad.
BOËTHIUS, A. M. S.: *Školská výchova*. In: BOËTHIUS. *Poslední Říman*. 1982, Praha: Vyšehrad.
CARR, B.: Úvod do metafyziky, 2004, Bratislava: Iris.
COMTE, A.: Kurz pozitívnej filozofie. In: Malá antológia z diel filozofov II, 1998, Bratislava: Slovenské pedagogické nakladateľstvo.
CONDORCET, J.A.: Náčrt historického obrazu pokroků lidského ducha, 1968, Praha: Academia.
DÉMUTH, A.: Teórie percepcie, 2013, Trnava: FFTU.
DOLISTA, J.:, Kognícia v morálnom správaní, 2013, Trnava: FFTU.
ELIADE, M.: Mýtus o věčném návratu, 2009, Praha: OIKOYMENH.
GÁLIKOVÁ, S.: Úvod do filozofie mysle, 2001, Bratislava: Honner.
GOFF, J.: Encyklopedie středověku, 2002, Praha: Vyšehrad.
GOODMAN, N.: Způsoby světatvorby, 1996, Bratislava: Archa.
HEGEL, G. W. F.: Filozofia dejín, 1957, Bratislava: Slovenské vydavateľstvo politickej literatúry.

HEIDEGGER, M.: *Co je to – filosofie?*, In: HEIDEGGER, M.: Básnicky bydlí člověk, 2006, Praha: OIKOYMENH.
HEIDEGGER, M.: Věk obrazu světa. In: Orientace, r.4, č. 5, 1969.
HERDER, J.G.: Vývoj lidskosti,1941, Praha: Jan Laichter.
JASPERS, K.: Malá škola filozofického myslenia, 2002, Bratislava: Kalligram.
JASPERS, K.: Úvod do filozofie, 1996, Praha: OIKOYMENH.
KANT, I.: Idey k všeobecným dejinám v svetoobčianskom zmysle. In: KANT, I.: K večnému mieru, 1996, Bratislava: Archa.
KIS, J.: Současná politická filosofie, 1997, Praha: OIKOYMENH.
KIŠOŇOVÁ, R.: Kognícia v sociálnom kontexte, 2013, Trnava: FFTU.
KIŠOŇOVÁ, R.: Kognitívna estetika, 2013, Trnava: FFTU.
LEMON, M.C.: Philosophy of History, 2003, London: Routledge.
MACHIAVELLI, N.: Vladař., 2007, Praha: Nakladatelství XYZ.
MARCELLI, M.: Filozofi v meste, 2008, Bratislava: Kalligram.
NIETZSCHE, F.: Nečasové úvahy I, 1993, Praha: Mladá fronta.
NIETZSCHE, F.: Tak vravel Zarathustra. Olomouc: Votobia, 1992.
NIETZSCHE, F.: Zrození tragedie, 1993, Praha: Gryf.
PATOČKA, J.: Kacířské eseje o filosofii dějin, 1990, Praha: Academia.
PATOČKA, J.: Vznik filosofie, 1991, In: Mýtus, epos, logos, Praha: OIKOYMENH.
PEREGRIN,J.: Filosofie pro normální lidi, 2008, Praha: Dokořán.
PIEPER, J.: *Co znamená filosofovat?* 2007, Kostelní Vydří: Karmelitánské nakladatelství.
POPPER, K.R.: Bída historicismu, 1994, Praha : OIKOYMENH.
PORUBJAK, M.: Vôľa (k) celku. Človek a spoločenstvo rečou Homéra a Theognida. 2010, Pusté Úľany: Schola Philosophica.
PTÁČKOVÁ, B.,Stibral, K.: Estetika, 2002, Praha: Rubico.
RICKERT, H.: Kultúrna veda a prírodná veda. In.: Antológia z diel filozofov. Zv. VII. 1967.
SCHMIDINGER, H.: Úvod do metafyziky, 2012, Praha: OIKOYMENH.
SOLOMON, R. C.: Filozofia ako problém? Radosť z filozofie: Abstraktné myslenie a vášnivý život: Večné problémy filozofie, 2004, Bratislava: Kalligram.
SPENGLER, O.: Zánik Západu. Obrysy morfológie světových dějin, 2011, Praha: Academia.

THURNHER, RÖD, SCHMIDINGER: Filosofie 19. a 20. století, 2009, Praha: OIKOYMENH.
TRAJTELOVÁ, J.: Kognitívna antropológia, 2013, Trnava: FFTU.
TRESMONTANT, C.: Bible a antická tradice, 1998, Praha: Vyšehrad.
VEYNE, P.: Jak se píšou dějiny, 2010, Praha: Pavel Merhart.
VICO, G.: Základy nové vědy o společné přirozenosti národů., 1991, Praha: Academia.
VIŠŇOVSKÝ, E. : *Filozofia ako problém? Filozofické poradenstvo ako forma filozofickej praxe: O životnej filozofii*, 2004, Bratislava: Kalligram.
ZIGO, M.: August Comte. In: Malá antológia z diel filozofov II., 1998, Bratislava: Slovenské pedagogické nakladateľstvo.

Renáta Kišoňová studied Philosophy at the University of Trnava. Her research interests include the problems of metaphysics.

www.ingramcontent.com/pod-product-compliance
Ingram Content Group UK Ltd.
Pitfield, Milton Keynes, MK11 3LW, UK
UKHW021322180426
11947UKWH00017B/1388